Long-Term Investments

Long-Term Investments

Project Planning and Appraisal

Srinivasan Sunderasan, Ph. D

LONDON AND NEW YORK

First published 2010 by Routledge

2 Park Square, Milton Park, Abingdon, Oxfordshire OX14 4RN
52 Vanderbilt Avenue, New York, NY 10017

Routledge is an imprint of the Taylor & Francis Group, an informa business

First issued in paperback 2019

Transferred to Digital Printing 2010

Typeset by
Mukesh Technologies Private Limited
#10, 2nd Floor
100 Feet Road
Ellapillaichavadi
Puducherry 605 005
India

British Library Cataloguing-in-Publication Data
A catalogue record of this book is available from the British Library

ISBN 13: 978-0-415-55604-0 (hbk)
ISBN 13: 978-0-367-17651-8 (pbk)

Contents

Preface

Project finance is not intensely researched owing to real world difficulties: most project companies, by definition, are private companies, owned by select individual and institutional shareholders ("concentrated ownership"). Consequently, little information is available in the public domain. Information released simultaneous with the issue of project-specific bonds, for instance, does not provide details required for academic inquiry. Further, each project faces a unique set of circumstances and hence projects do not lend themselves to rigorous statistical analyses. They are, therefore, studied as isolated cases, and the lessons thus drawn are not readily transferable.

The limited text material available to highlight the relationships among capital structure, managerial incentives and valuation has also constrained teaching efforts at business schools. *Long-term Investments* is intended to give a bird's eye view of projects for a diverse audience encountered at contemporary business schools. This book is an attempt to blend the theory from Corporate Finance courses with the real world situations encountered by a project analyst. It provides a systematic 'guided-tour' of the world of projects commencing with a strategic view, through the development of financial models and culminates with an evaluation of risk and the design of risk-mitigation measures. Given the emphasis on the development of financial models to help make investment decisions, it is designed to simultaneously appeal to business school students and to serve as a do-it-yourself guide for practicing professionals.

The strength of the present offering is its focus on long-term, large-scale investment projects. It starts with the basic concepts, helping the reader grasp the subject gradually and systematically, culminating with the application of these concepts to real-life situations.

Srinivasan Sunderasan
May 2009

Appraisal of Large-Scale Investment Projects: An Overview

KEY CHAPTER CONCEPTS

1. A project is a major undertaking with a predefined set of activities aimed at achieving a specified goal within a prescribed time horizon.

2. Project companies are constituted to mobilize and deploy resources to create and operate project-specific assets.

3. While there may not be a universal definition, projects involving US$ 100 million or more in investments and 15 years or more of anticipated useful lives, could be considered "large" in scale.

4. Investment decision making involves detailed investigations to ascertain the risks affecting the business transaction and putting appropriate mitigation measures in place.

GLOSSARY OF NEW TERMS

Asset specificity transaction-specific, non-redeployable assets that are destined to perform unique tasks within the project.

Debt Service payment of principal and interest on a loan

Leverage the ratio of debt to total owners' capital.

Limited liability the liability of a firm's investors limited to the capital invested.

Non-recourse debt Debt that is serviced exclusively by the cash-flows emanating from the operations of the project company.

Project Company A legal entity incorporated to undertake the tasks comprising the project.

Risk contamination the phenomenon whereby a failing project imposes additional risks on an otherwise healthy sponsor.

Sponsor (and collectively sponsors) the project's equity owner(s).

Remaining Afloat: Project Decision Making Challenge

On January 12 2004, the Queen Mary 2 (QM2) set sail on her maiden voyage from Southampton, England to Fort Lauderdale, Florida in the United States, carrying 2,620 passengers. The QM2 is undoubtedly the most magnificent ocean liner ever built, studded with opulent public areas, lavishly appointed dining rooms, ballrooms, theatres, lounges, kennels and the one of a kind planetarium at sea.

Ocean liner company, Cunard*, have put their experience from over a century and a half to good use in concocting a singular blend of the old-world charm of seafaring with exalted luxury to serve the world's elite, ranging from royalty and statesmen to rock artists and film stars. The US$800m ocean liner, specifically designed for the challenging transatlantic routes required 40% more steel than a comparable cruise liner, and a power plant capable of propelling the ship at about 30 knots, considered essential to wean traffic away from modern day super jumbos. At a capacity of about 2,600 guests, the capital cost of

---

*   *www.cunard.com;*

(*Continued*)

constructing the ocean liner is estimated at US$300,000 per berth: twice the previous benchmark for cruise ships.

Everything about the QM2 is spectacular, including the crew size of 1253 personnel. In fact, Cunard has consciously decided not to restrict her size to PANAMAX standards – the largest ship dimension passing through the Panama Canal, and as she is too large to dock in most ports, passengers are ferried to and from the ship.

The Queen Mary 2 is a product of meticulous appraisal and conscious financial decision making. Decisions such as the commissioning of the QM2 project affect the risk of the firm and the success of the firm in maximizing shareholder wealth. Among the key concerns for decision makers are:

- Cash-flow considerations – optimizing revenues from operations to justify the first cost, recover the operational expenditure and to earn respectable returns for shareholders within an acceptable timeframe.

- Capital structure decisions – mobilizing investment resources and appropriately sizing the debt and equity components in keeping with the cashflow patterns for the project.

- Risk assessment and mitigation – estimating and minimizing the uncertainty associated with future cashflows at least cost.

The financial concepts and tools needed to deal with such concerns in various settings, and to help make more effective decisions are the subject matter of this book. Given the huge demand for investments, especially into infrastructure projects in several developing countries, investors, finance managers, lawyers, consultants, and officials involved in rolling out, operating and regulating such projects need to be adequately equipped to structure transactions so as to maximise value and minimise risk of failure.

Introduction

A project* is typically a major undertaking contemplated as comprising a unique set of predefined tasks, intended to achieve a preset goal within a prescribed time horizon.

A project normally involves the setup of a legally independent, limited liability project company, with its own management structure, personnel and corporate governance systems. The project company raises equity capital from one or more sources and supplements it with non-recourse debt for creation of specified capital assets. Project finance is, essentially, the process of allocating project risk to the entities that are most suited to managing them. Most projects involve large upfront capital costs and very low operating costs relative to the upfront costs. In other words, typical project investments have a "time profile", that is, most of the costs are borne up-front, while benefits from the project are derived with a delay. Additionally, most project companies have few investment opportunities for the free cash generated. The most common applications of project finance are in resource extraction and infrastructure sectors.

The Project Company

Project Financing is the process of mobilizing funding for large capital-intensive projects, *inter alia*, involving the creation of project specific assets with finite lives to be owned and managed by the project company. A project company typically has few—often in the order of three — sponsors, who then approach lenders to mobilize project debt. A limited liability project company avoids risk contamination i.e., insulates the sponsoring parent in the event of the project's failure.

---

*   Literally: something thrown forward: derived from Latin *pro - "forward"* and *jacere - "to throw"*, Harper, *(2001), Online Etymology Dictionary* , http://dictionary.reference.com/browse/project.

The creation of a legally distinct entity to acquire, own and operate the assets created for the project imparts focus. The expenditure incurred by the project company is readily mapped on to investments flowing in, enhancing transparency in cash-flows and hence superior oversight of free-cashflow management.

A legal entity with a distinct physical location is also suited to effect the installation of a custom-designed management structure, tailored to deliver on the project's objectives. Issues relating to corporate governance, information sharing and expeditious decision making are better addressed and resolved within the framework of a project company.

Non-recourse Debt

The most distinctive feature of project finance is the lenders' exclusive dependence on the project's cash flows to service the project company's debt. In project parlance, the term "Project Finance" is frequently used to synonymously with non-recourse debt. As a natural extension of this feature, the lenders also rely solely on the project assets as security against the loan. In the event of default, the lenders could choose to enforce their security interests and liquidate or otherwise restructure project assets to recover the debt service due. Loan contracts are generally structured such that in the event of willful neglect, fraud, misrepresentation of facts, or incomplete disclosure of material information by the sponsor, lenders have access to the sponsors' other assets. Under these conditions, as lenders have some recourse to assets held outside of the project company, the debt is referred to as limited recourse financing.

Project companies typically have highly leveraged capital structures. Debt to total capital employed could reach 70 per cent in certain cases, often limited only by the ability of the project to generate the cash required to service the debt. The sponsors transfer the major portion of the project risk to debt holders, who are presumed to be better placed to assume and manage such risk. Lenders contribute the largest proportion of the investment in the project and therefore absorb the highest risk, and yet receive fixed (or capped) returns on their investments. Since the debt holders depend completely on the success of the project, they impose rigorous discipline on management through binding contracts and effective oversight through periodic audits. Contracts normally also mandate project companies to route their cash flows through lender banks to ensure debt service on priority. High leverage helps sponsors reduce their own equity commitments and such oversight by the lenders also provides sponsors with an additional layer of supervision, especially in situations where ownership and management of the project company are separated.

Project Categories

Business propositions appropriately suited for project financing are those which indicate stable and reasonably predictable cash flow patterns. Such projects broadly fall into two categories:

- Flow type projects: this group of projects depends on the flow of business, typically traffic through the project asset to be created viz., toll roads, railway and power transmission lines, telecom networks, gas or oil pipelines etc., and the project's ability to service debt and earn a return for investors depends on traffic volumes and the evolution of usage tariff over time. Pricing for carriage in flow-type projects is generally determined by the willingness to pay within the local context.

- Stock-type projects: mines, oil and gas reserves and other such natural endowments are extracted in a phased manner and the proceeds from their sale go towards debt service and towards earning returns for shareholders. While quantity extracted is constrained by capacity of project assets and associated logistics, pricing in most such situations is determined by the global supply and demand patterns for the commodity in question. In certain circumstances, the quantity extracted itself determines, and is reciprocally influenced by, the prevailing market price, as in the case of international crude oil supplies. The stock-type project ends simultaneously with the depletion of the mineral, oil or other reserve.

Large projects of either category invariably yield social, economic and environmental externalities which would need to be assessed and managed appropriately. Social impacts such as the need for displacement and rehabilitation of people from potential mining or construction project sites, and environmental spillovers including soil and ground water degradation and deforestation would have to be planned for. While the definition of a large project could be context-specific, in general, a project involving over US$ 100 million in investments and having an anticipated useful life of over 15 years could be termed a large-scale project.

A "mega-project" is said to involve investments in excess of US$ 1 billion, with an anticipated useful life of over 50 years. Prolonged lifespans add to the uncertainty associated with the predictions for market demand and pricing of the services sought to be offered. Such projects typically involve the acquisition of large tracts of land or common property resources which would necessitate the active participation of the state in the mega project. In response, the state also provides a launch aid or 'viability gap funding' to help compensate for the indirect benefits accruing to society consequent to project implementation, the value of which the project company would otherwise not be in a position to capture.

Table 1.1 lays out the steps involved in rolling out a project, where the need for the service and hence the business opportunity are identified by the government agency concerned. This is common in the context of stock type projects such as oil fields, coal deposits or in select cases in flow type projects such as those intended to harness hydro electric power, construction of large motorways etc. The traditional approach has also involved the constitution of special purpose state-owned enterprises (SOE) to undertake implementation and to deliver services.

Table 1.1: Conventional Approach to Project Development*

i.   Identify alternatives (government);

ii.   Draft terms of reference and recruit consultants for feasibility study (government);

iii.   Undertake feasibility study (consultants): preliminary design, and cost estimates; market analysis; economic analysis; financial analysis;

iv.   Draft terms of reference and recruit consultants to evaluate safety aspects related to different alternatives (government);

v.   Carry out safety study (consultants): impact on and requirements with respect to road traffic and passenger safety; impact and requirements with respect to maritime safety;

vi.   Draft terms of reference and recruit consultants to undertake environmental impact study (government);

vii.   Undertake project appraisal, and make recommendation to government (government);

viii.   Make decision (government). Supplementary studies may have to be carried out before a decision can be made;

ix.   Establish SOE to implement project;

x.   Application for required permits (first phase; approval of preliminary design), including the preparation of necessary documentation to obtain permits (SOE);

xi.   Mobilise finance (SOE; government);

xii.   Recruit consultants to prepare detailed design and for supervision (SOE);

xiii.   Preparation of detailed design (consultants);

xiv.   Application for required permits (second phase; approval of detailed design) (SOE);

xv.   Recruit contractors (SOE);

xvi.   Supervise (consultants);

xvii.   Commission and initiate operations.

---

*   *Reproduced with permission from Elsevier. Rothengatter, Flyvbjerg and Bruzelius (2002)*

Tables 1.2 and 1.3 differ from table 1.1 above in that a pre-feasibility study is undertaken to ensure *prima facie* viability of the project while project implementation itself could be carried out either by a private entity or a state owned enterprise. In the light of the difficulties with large-scale displacement, possible social unrest and the costs involved in resettlement and rehabilitation, Rothengatter et al. (2002) have also suggested widespread consultations with stakeholders.

Table 1.3 provides the logical progression towards implementation of a project through a specially constituted state-owned enterprise, also referred to as a public-sector enterprise. This could be a route taken where the services in question are best provided by monopoly

Table 1.2: Approach to project development with private sector project implementation

i.	Undertake a policy study and publish a policy document. To be done by government;
ii.	Prepare terms of reference and recruit consultants to draft performance specifications. To be done by government;
iii.	Prepare draft performance specifications. To be done by consultants, commissioned by government, based on government policy objectives, laws and regulations;
iv.	Prepare terms of reference and recruit consultants to prepare a pre-feasibility study. To be done by government;
v.	Prepare terms of reference and recruit consultants to prepare plan for involvement of the public (public hearings, interest group involvement, peer review, etc.). To be done by government;
vi.	Prepare pre-feasibility study. To be done by consultants, commissioned by government. If the prefeasibility study indicates an unfeasible project, the process may stop here;
vii.	Prepare Consultation Document 1. To be done by government. Will be used for wide consultation with the public;
viii.	Carry out consultation with public and regulatory bodies;
ix.	Prepare terms of reference (government) and recruit consultants to propose regulatory regime, carry out further analysis of access links and the associated costs, make proposals for the operations of a possible fixed link, etc.
x.	Prepare Consultation Document 2. To be done by government. Will be used for wide consultation with the public;
xi.	Prepare Final Performance Specification Document;

(Continued)

Table 1.2: (Cont'd)

xii. Prepare Decision Document. To be done by government and will identify. Mode of operation; tender procedures, if relevant; regulatory regime. Cost estimates and financing conditions for access links.

xiii. Develop necessary legislation and make decision in Parliament to stop or go ahead with the project;

xiv. If project is ratified, undertake pre-qualification of bidders. To be done by government with the assistance of consultants;

xv. Prepare short-list and ask for bids. To be done by government with the assistance of consultants;

xvi. Evaluate bids, including acceptance from a performance point of view. To be done by government, including relevant regulatory bodies; if no bids are received, or bids are received that do not meet performance specifications, and it transpires that the bidders are not prepared to modify their bids to ensure performance in terms of those specifications, then the process stops due to non-performance;

xvii. Select and negotiate and sign preliminary agreement;

xviii. Prepare and circulate Information Document. To be done by government. Publication will be subject to review by Auditor General. With the publication of the Information Document, the time has come when the selected operator can initiate preparation of final designs in order to obtain (i) final permits from regulatory authorities and (ii) bids from contractors;

xix. Submit negotiated agreement for approval and signature by relevant authorities and concessionaire;

xx. Prepare detailed design and obtain final clearance from relevant environmental and safety authorities, If clearance cannot be obtained, the project may be terminated at this stage;

xxi. Implement agreement;

xxii. Monitor and audit agreement.

Table 1.3: Approach to project development with private sector project implementation

i. Undertake a policy study and publish a policy document. To be done by government;

ii. Prepare terms of reference and recruit consultants to draft performance specifications. To be done by government;

(Continued)

Table 1.3: (Cont'd)

iii.	Prepare draft performance specifications. To be done by consultants, commissioned by government, based on government policy objectives, laws and regulations;
iv.	Prepare terms of reference and recruit consultants to prepare a pre-feasibility study. To be done by government;
v.	Prepare terms of reference and recruit consultants to prepare plan for involvement of the public (public hearings, interest group involvement, peer review, etc.). To be done by government;
vi.	Prepare pre-feasibility study. To be done by consultants, commissioned by government. If the pre-feasibility study indicates an unfeasible project, the process may stop here;
vii.	Prepare Consultation Document 1. To be done by government. Will be used for wide consultation with the public;
viii.	Carry out consultation with public and regulatory bodies;
ix.	Prepare terms of reference (government) and recruit consultants to propose regulatory regime, carry out further analysis of access links and the associated costs, make proposals for the operations of a possible fixed link, etc.
x.	Prepare Consultation Document 2. To be done by government. Will be used for wide consultation with the public;
xi.	Prepare Final Performance Specification Document;
xii.	Prepare Decision Document. To be done by government and will identify. Mode of operation; tender procedures, if relevant; regulatory regime. Cost estimates and financing conditions for access links.
xiii.	Develop necessary legislation and make decision in Parliament to stop or go ahead with the project;
xiv.	If project is ratified, establish SOE;
xv.	Identify financial performance requirements to be met by the SOE and negotiate a preliminary agreement regarding these requirements. Preliminary agreement to be signed by government and SOE. If agreement cannot be reached the project may be terminated at this stage;
xvi.	Require SOE to negotiate and reach a preliminary agreement with potential financiers of fixed connection. If agreement cannot be reached the project may be terminated at this stage;

(Continued)

Table 1.3: (Cont'd)

xvii.	Prepare and circulate Information Document. To be done by government. Publication will be subject to review by Auditor General;
xviii.	Submit negotiated agreement between government and SOE for ratification and signature by relevant authorities and SOE;
xix.	Implement agreement;
xx.	Monitor and audit agreement.

service providers and regulation of a private-sector monopoly could be unviable. In theory, the state-owned enterprise helps balance the government's social and economic objectives by providing services at the least cost possible while remaining adequately liquid.

Participants Involved in a Project Scheme

Figure 1.1 is a schematic illustration of the various actors involved in project implementation and operation. Evidently, the project set-up involves the institution of multiple contracts involving disparate legal entities. The project financing and implementing structure is often referred to as a "nexus of contracts".

The sponsors spot a viable opportunity and invite consultants and investment bankers to help package it into business proposition. When multiple sponsors are involved, their respective rights and obligations are defined under the terms of the shareholders' agreement. The investment bankers also help attract external equity investments and debt financing for the proposed project. Depending on the magnitude of the project, specialized risk-management consultants could be appointed to procure appropriate insurance and other contracts for the project. Even as it appears that project financing and implementation involve preparation of several contracts and allied documents, the substance of these instruments is determined by the Project Analyst, basing on detailed financial models and projected future states of the world.

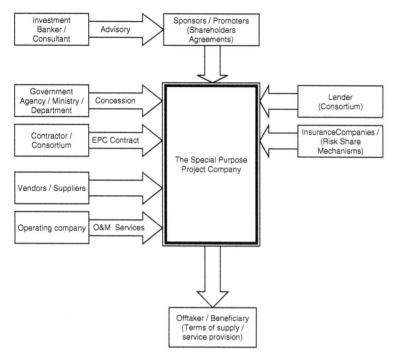

Figure 1.1: Participants in Project Financing and Implementation

Necessary statutory approvals and rights to implement the project are sought from the government authorities and agencies concerned. The Engineering-Procurement-Construction (EPC) contractor is then appointed to design and implement the project. The involvement of an EPC contractor also serves as the first line of defence in case of delays in implementation, as the EPC contracts typically require the contractor to compensate the project for revenue lost due to delays, unsatisfactory workmanship etc. Similarly, other vendors are held liable for the quality of supplies and are accountable for departure from agreed timelines. In road related and other real estate projects, typically, an operating company is appointed to manage the project asset created and to generate revenues from providing services to the offtaker or the ultimate beneficiary. Other projects such as power plants, where skills required for operations and maintenance are highly specialized and relatively scarce, are managed by in-house personnel.

The Project Financial Appraisal Function

Project appraisal and investment decision-making warrants a curious combination of skills, ranging from strategic foresight to a thorough understanding of the nitty-gritty of applicable taxation laws and the like. Practitioners are required to understand the complex relationship among the project structure, the environment, managerial incentives and value creation. This is compounded by the fact that individual projects are faced with a unique set of circumstances with little or no overlap with other projects. In effect, each large project is a case study and has to be dealt with in isolation. The amount, timing and certainty of the cashflows generated by the project are determined by the key financial management decisions including the capital structure, financing decisions, ownership structure decisions and dividend decisions, made within the context of the prevailing and projected macroeconomic environment.

The elementary sub-task within the appraisal mandate is the creation of a robust financial model, comprising the income statement, balance sheet and the statement of cash-flows for the proposed project. Such modeling calls for financial accounting skills combined with the detailed and updated information on the applicable taxes and the tax discounts and waivers, if any, provided for the given class of projects. The financial model is subject to rigorous analyses to enlist the best and worst future states for the project. For contemporary projects, this is conveniently and rapidly accomplished through the use of spreadsheet software. Financial planning then involves the prioritisation of the alternative sources of long-term funds, viz., issuance of project specific bonds, syndicated debt from banking channels etc.

Upon receipt of requisite approvals, sanctions and statutory clearances, the detailed legal documentation is prepared, contracts are executed and the project is implemented. Risk management involves the reallocation of perceived risks to insurance companies, contractors or other counter parties who are better equipped to bear them. The project is closely monitored through construction and operation to confirm adherence to the plans. Alternatively, if corrective action is warranted the financial model is updated to optimize the project for the renewed circumstances.

Organization of this Text

This text provides an introduction to both the analytical tools and the descriptive materials employed in appraising long-term projects, intended to acquaint the reader with the circumstances facing financial decision makers and help develop a framework for systematic decision-making. The subject matter is structured as follows:

Strategic aspects of project evaluation: An end-to-end perspective to enable a rapid assessment of the proposed project including a study of spill over effects beyond the project boundary.

Preparation of a Financial Model: Drawing up the revenue model with specific assumptions, and preparation of the income statement, the balance sheet and the statement of cashflows.

Means of Finance: Optimal capital structure decisions in keeping with cashflow patterns and tax structures.

Investment Appraisal: Various measures to compute the return on investment from the project, and investment decision making based on acceptability thresholds.

Analysis of Risk: Sensitivity and Scenario Analyses, Simulation and analyses of probability density.

Risk Management: Portfolio risk, interest rate risk, foreign exchange risk, managed through hedging, options, insurance contracts and other instruments.

Although the subject matter in this text is laid out in distinct parts to impart a certain order, the various decisions are interrelated and potentially circular: for instance, different risk management measures could alter cash-flow patterns in different ways. Similarly, various combinations of debt and equity comprising the capital investment could yield distinct cash-flow patterns. Conversely, the cash-flow patterns of the project have the potential of influencing the risk management and capital strucutre decisions. Discussions are laced with mention of relevant case situations to highlight project financial management issues.

References

Cunard, http://www.cruiseweb.com/CUNARD-QUEEN-MARY-2.HTM and http://en.wikipedia.org/wiki/Queen_Mary_2

Rothengatter Werner, Flyvbjerg Bent and Bruzelius, Nils "Big Decisions, Big Risks. Improving Accountability in Mega Projects", Transport Policy, Vol. 9, Issue 2, April 2002, p 143 – 154.

Strategic Aspects of Large-scale Investment Projects

KEY CHAPTER CONCEPTS

1. A system-wide view of the project enables the financial manager make strategic decisions relating to the environment within which the project is expected to perform.

2. One-of-a-kind and first-of-its-kind projects are associated with a greater magnitude of uncertainty compared to modular and repetitive projects.

3. Even as businesses compete to cut costs in a globalized world, considerations relating to country of origin and business environment determine project location and hence influence eventual outcomes.

4. A disciplined and objective due diligence assessment helps uncover vital information and helps optimize the project for various future states.

GLOSSARY OF NEW TERMS

Annuity a series of equal cash flows per period for a specified duration.

Capital investment expenditure made on purchase of long-term assets, expected to yield future cash benefits.

Due diligence systematic examination and evaluation of risks affecting a proposed investment.

Liquidity the firm's ability to meet short-term financial obligations.

Scenario Analysis undertaken to determine the outcome of a simultaneous change in several input parameters.

Sensitivity Analysis undertaken to determine the outcome of a change in one of the input parameters, holding other inputs constant.

Solvency the firm's ability to meet contracted financial obligations as they come due.

Slippery Slopes: Challenges in Project Implementation

"If it weren't so pathetic, it would have been almost comical", writes Donald Trump referring to the inadequacies, the six year delay and the $13 million spent on several attempts at renovating the Wollman ice-skating rink in Central Park, New York, one of the largest man-made skating rinks in the United States of America. Eventually, Trump managed to complete the construction of the rink in less than four months, at a cost of just over US$ 2 million, in what when on to be billed as the contrast between governmental incompetence and the power of effective private enterprise[*].

In 1980 New York City closed the rink for renovations, which were expected to take no longer than two years. "The city originally

---

[*]   *Trump (1987)*

(*Continued*)

estimated that the repair bill would total $9 million, but it eventually reached $12 million without a cube of ice to show for it. The roof of the pavilion, which houses the changing rooms and restaurant, was riddled with holes and made a perfect sieve. The ice-making equipment could not do its job because its 22 miles of refrigeration pipes had sprung dozens of leaks, a disaster that was not discovered until after concrete had been poured. The pipes were further damaged as workmen chopped up the concrete to make repairs. The rink's floor was also badly slanted, causing water to accumulate at one end[†]."

The divergent methods employed by Trump and the Parks Department of the New York City administration showed up in stark contrast. Trump hired Toronto, based Cimco, acknowledged as the best among ice skating rink builders, as consultants and equipment suppliers. He was also able to pay the contractors and suppliers as soon as the work was completed. Trump was free to pay overtime to meet his deadline, an incentive seldom allowed in government contracts. Most important of all, as a private entrepreneur, Donald Trump could make decisions in minutes, and on the spot, while the governmental machinery could take up to two years for the same. As a result, in a single week, the crew installed the 22 miles of piping required and tested it for leaks and then in one day, 290 people poured concrete until the entire floor was done.

Government departments in most countries are clearly in a bind, charged with the immense responsibility of creating public assets with public resources, yet having to follow standard operating procedures and to tread with caution at each stage. In the United States, for instance, on any contract above $50,000, a regulation called the Wick's Law says that a minimum of four contractors must be invited, with the business going to the lowest bidders. Clearly, the lowest bidders may not necessarily be the best performers. Trump used the best in the business as consultants, as equipment suppliers and as construction contractors, largely through sole source procurement. Further, Trump could make spot decisions while the City had to go through the chain of command to seek approvals.

[†]   *DeMott (1986)*

Introduction

Successful project appraisal mandates an encyclopedic knowledge of operations to be instituted and simultaneously, and certainly more importantly, the ability to envision the project from 30,000 feet. Such dual perspectives give the financial manager the credibility to make far-reaching investment decisions, (Hill and Wetlaufer, 1998).

Projects with greater public ownership, larger, first-of-its-kind and one-of-a-kind projects generally exhibit worse performance. Adequate provision needs to be made for project delays, technology malfunction and budget overruns. Ostensibly, isolated, technology intensive projects face uncertainty levels that are far greater than repetitive, modular projects. While financing plays a significant part in the success of a project, in several instances, strategic perspectives determine the eventual outcome. Reichardt (2007) cautions that neglecting non-financial risk in areas such as environmental, socio-economic and sustainability performance could potentially be disastrous, particularly in developing countries. The prevailing macro-economic environment, the nature of government and governance, the speed of decision making, taxation and enforceability of contracts are vital considerations. This is then followed by project specific evaluation, of the value chain and other components of the ecosystem, of the competition and of the customers.

The Regulatory Environment

Gomes, Kotlikoff and Viceira (2007) observe that government indecision and delays in policy making distort economic choices and impose a large burden on people. While quantifying the excess burden of government indecision, it is emphasized that the economic loss is incurred *not* from implementing specific policy initiatives but from delaying their determination and announcement.

The cost of policy uncertainty and the benefits of responsive regulation are observed in both categories of projects: stock type as well as flow type. China, for instance, has initiated a series of measures to ensure adequate supply of minerals and mineral products to feed its rapidly growing economy. Despite the Chinese government's concerted efforts, the overall level of investment in mining projects by foreign enterprises remains small. Suxun and Chenjunnan (2008) perceive that private investment into China's mining and minerals industry is discouraged by the uncertainty associated with the mineral rights and the lack of investment security. A potential investor is likely to abstain from investing in an environment where government departments participate in business activity, while the government also remains a business regulator. It is observed that private entrepreneurs in China face more stringent laws and regulations in terms of access to the minerals industry and constantly face intrusions from local governments and worse, threats of takeover of their enterprises by their larger government owned counterparts.

Investors seek to invest in projects operating within environments where applicable policy is transparent, fair and consistent, regardless of ownership, scale of operations and the like. Investors would require a reasonable assurance of security of their rights as a pre-condition to making the investment. Upon evaluating data relating to forty developing economies, over the decade of the 1990s, Banerjee, Oetzel and Ranganathan (2006) confirm that the volume and frequency of private investment in infrastructure are definitely impacted by institutional structures and bureaucratic quality.

Country of Origin and Branding Decisions

In a globalized world, where production processes have been disintegrated and as trade in finished product has given way to 'trade in tasks', tasks that are best kept close to home remain onshore while other tasks are shifted to lower-cost places offshore. Such vertical disintegration and the consequent dispersion of production are hailed beneficial for all concerned, (Economist[b], 2007). A notable departure has been sports car maker, Porsche's decision to buck the trend and erect a substantial plant in Leipzig, Eastern Germany, for its new sports utility vehicle, the *Cayenne*, despite the fact that wages in Germany are higher than those in Eastern Europe by a factor of six or seven. The Cayenne has gone on to become the company's best selling model ever and its success is largely attributed to its "Made in Germany" tag, (Lagace, 2006). While some part of the unorthodox decision is explained by the higher productivity of the German work force, it is believed that German companies compete as niche producers on the strength of their legendary engineering, craftsmanship and quality.

Once the decision to base a project is made, project analysts evaluate project specific aspects. In this context, we look at peculiar risks associated with certain categories of projects.

Very Large Projects

Airbus, a European Aeronautic Defence and Space Company EADS. N.V. (EADS) company[*], officially handed over the first super jumbo, the Airbus A380, to Singapore Airlines on October 15, 2007. Equipped with 471 seats spread over three passenger classes, the spacious jetliner's commissioning was hailed as the beginning of a new chapter in civil aviation. The company also announced that the deliveries of 189 additional aircraft to 16 customers including Emirates Airlines and Qantas, besides Singapore Airlines, were on track. USA Today (2008) reported that by March 2008, Singapore Airlines had to temporarily ground the two Airbus A380 aircraft in service to sort out technical glitches with the fuel pump.

Technical difficulties and consequent delays have plagued the Airbus A380 project from the start. The October 2007 delivery to Singapore Airlines was already over 18 months behind schedule.

---

[*]   *www.airbus.com*

Several airline companies and cargo carriers had cancelled orders compounding the misery. Initial production delays were attributed to the complexity from having to install 100,000 wires and 40,300 connectors adding up to 530km of wiring in each aircraft. The cumulative earnings shortfall through 2010 is estimated at €4.8 billion. The EADS stock price took a pounding and forced several changes among the top management.

The decision to build an important new "game–changer" product invariably means "betting the company". With the A380, Airbus has risked everything to create an enduring icon to capture the imagination of air travelers, the world over, (Economist[c], 2007). The Airbus A380 is no exception as far as delays and budget overruns are concerned. The revolutionary Boeing 787 Dreamliner project is also behind schedule due to the shortage of aluminum fasteners and due to problems with its flight-control software. Projects such as the development of the dreamliner and the super jumbo could be frustrating on account of their massive scale, sophistication and sheer complexity. For instance, some of the structural components of the A380 are transported to the assembly hall in Toulouse, France by surface, sections of the fuselage travel the roll-on/roll-off ship and the wings ride a barge. Owing to the size of the components in question, new wider roads, canal systems and barges were developed to deliver the parts.

As a result of the delays, the additional infrastructure creation and the cancellations, the breakeven production volume for the A380 has been pushed beyond the originally computed figure of 420 aircraft, in a restricted market environment. Even as strategic considerations relating to ending rival Boeing's monopoly on the large aircraft segment are at play, and given the expected revenue streams from maintenance and repair of planes, analysts are, as yet, uncertain on whether the project investment estimated at about €20 billion would eventually prove worthwhile. The super jumbo is a typical case of a very large project that could potentially pull a company down owing to its sheer magnitude, complexity and the larger than anticipated outlay on contingencies.

Public Works

As evident from the case summary relating to the ice-skating rink at the beginning of this chapter, implementation of projects by the public-sector suffers generic structural flaws. While larger projects require greater coordination and are hence likely to run over time and over budget, public projects suffer from dithering and lax decision making. For example, the ten mile long metro rail in Calcutta (later renamed Kolkata), India, took twenty two years to build and its budget was revised upward fourteen times. Morris (1990) observes that the involvement of multiple public sector units leads to a 'vicious circle of delays', initiated in each unit by poor project design and implementation, inadequate funding, bureaucratic indecision and lack of coordination among enterprises.

Yet, implementation of public projects is not always as slack. If the lack of leadership was cited by Donald Trump as the cause for the chaos in Central Park, career railway engineer E. Sridharan, of the Delhi Metro Rail Corporation (DMRC) has been an exception in an otherwise bureaucratic railway setup. Leading from the front, he demanded and secured full power to pick his team of professionals – including the right to fire. He has insisted on the global best in technology and equipment and is known to have worked tirelessly to remove every element of subjectivity in procurement processes, (Economist[a], 2006). As a result, the 56km metro network in the Indian national capital region of Delhi, was on budget and was completed nearly three years ahead of schedule, with an additional 53 km slated to be completed as planned, by the Summer of 2010. Effective leadership could significantly narrow the gap between public sector implementation and private enterprise. Further, timely implementation of public projects could set a precedent to attract private investment projects, as it signals the right environment for expeditious decision making.

One-of-a-Kind Projects

The Channel Tunnel linking the UK and France has been subjected to intense scrutiny for many years now. Initially hailed as an engineering wonder bringing the islands closer to the mainland through the under-sea link, Eurotunnel the company managing the infrastructure soon emerged as an iconic symbol of all that could go wrong with project finance.

Eurotunnel[†] operates truck shuttle and passenger shuttle (car and coach) services between Folkestone, UK and Calais, France and also earns toll revenue from train operators (Eurostar for rail passengers, and English Welsh and Scottish Railway (EWS) and SNCF—is the National Railway of France providing high speed train travel to Europe for rail freight) which use the Tunnel. The Eurotunnel has gone on record acknowledging that it faces "fundamental" financial difficulties and has consistently struggled to meet interest payments due on its debt. Passenger numbers through the tunnel have never lived up to expecta-tions. Eurostar trains carry about 6 million passengers a year compared to original forecasts of 16 million. Ferries have survived beyond the predicted expiry date, while budget carriers have made flying a more attractive option.

Vilanova (2006) concludes that Eurotunnel's distress stems from its inappropriately designed governance structure and principal-agent conflicts. Significantly, the author also goes on to suggest that lender banks chose to remain passive and not to press for bankruptcy proceed-ings despite the defaults, primarily to sustain their bargaining power within a firm in chronic financial distress, while avoiding having to write off the loans to the project.

With the benefit of hindsight, however, the project makes for an interesting study. Apart from the fact that the company was highly leveraged and that shareholding was dispersed among several indi-vidual investors, the assets created are highly specific and immovable. It is inconceivable that planners of a project of such epic proportions would have overlooked the threat of substitutes such as low-fare airlines and ferries and consequently the impact of such competition on pric-ing and traffic volumes. The illiquidity and the consequent defaults,

---

† *www.eurotunnel.com*

the agency problems detected and lender passivity are a natural corollary to low business volumes and such asset specificity. Additionally, the company was exposed to traffic revenue risk which could have been transferred to governments or insurance companies better equipped to absorb such risks, through, for instance, the development of contractual structures such as the annuity model, (Singh and Kalidindi, 2006), which would have capped such risk.

First-of-its-Kind Projects

Research and Development projects are exposed to acute uncertainties owing to their exploratory nature and the challenges involved in designing and building systems and sub-systems from existing or new components[‡].

The stationary south-facing hemi-spherical ferro-cement bowl, 15 meters in diameter and 7 meters above the ground, abutting the Solar kitchen in Auroville[§] is designed to harness the sun's rays and

---

‡   *Thomas Alva Edison is said to have made several unsuccessful attempts at designing the incandescent light bulb and to have remarked that he had successfully discovered thousand ways to not make a light bulb.*

§   *www.auroville.org*

focus on a cylindrical boiler which follows the sun's position by means of a computerized tracking device. The project is funded by the Indian government's Ministry of New and Renewable Energy. In all, over 11,000 pieces of hand cut, flat 3mm thick glass mirrors are placed to constitute the reflecting surface, which is sized to generate steam sufficient to cook 1000 meals on clear sunny days. The solar bowl has been hybridized with a conventional diesel fired boiler back-up system for cooking through a heat-storage tank designed to store heat for one hour. Throughout the year, approximately 700 lunches are prepared at the solar kitchen, of which, about 400 meals are packed and sent to Auroville's schools and service centers around 11.15 am.

The solar bowl, one of the largest concentrators of its type in the world, has been an experimental project and has several firsts to its credit, including a hemispherical profile as opposed to a conventional parabolic one, and the use of ordinary mirrors against custom made concave mirrors and other unconventional building materials and techniques.

Given the complexity of the computerized tracking arm and the one-off use of the thermic fluid for heat transfer and storage, technical hitches are generally anticipated, even welcomed to help innovate and improve on the project. While the technical details have captured people's imagination, investors seem to have overlooked an essential aspect of the project: the availability of the design quantity of steam at precisely the time when meals are to be prepared as early as 10.00 in the morning, to be in time to dispatch food to the schools. Obviously, this has not been the case. Further, the heat generated towards the end of the afternoon cannot be used to cook supper as the heat storage is limited to one hour.

Project appraisal should assess the end-to-end functionality along with the financial viability of the project. Such consistency and reliability assessments are vital in situations such as the prototype solar bowl discussed here, to facilitate large-scale replication. In addition to the financial and technical viability of the project on hand, the analysis should cover strategic and synergistic effects with correlated projects, social, political, environmental and technical linkages and other organisational issues, (Lopes and Flavell, 1998).

Due Diligence

The specificity of sizing, location and function of project related assets limit options for salvage and redeployment, as evident from the Eurotunnel and solar bowl cases discussed above. Under such circumstances, abandoning the project is not an option for investors. Lenders choose to remain passive and prefer not having to write-off project debts, as enforcement of security interests leads to minimal recoveries, if at all. Large projects viz., hydro electric power projects do not offer great scope for mid-course correction or reorientation, and if they do, the costs involved tend to be prohibitive. Once established, the opportunity to increase or reduce capacity for most projects could be severely limited. As most projects are go or no-go decisions, project analysts need to establish a firm basis for the design and to rigorously verify all assumptions prior to initiating activity on the ground.

The success of a project is inextricably linked to the meticulousness of the due diligence effort invested i.e, the care a prudent person is expected to exercise in the evaluation of risks affecting a proposed business transaction. Such due diligence investigation is usually carried out by a disinterested third party — consultants, auditors, lawyers and the like on behalf of a potential investor (or lender) intending to set-up a project or acquire existing project assets. The scrutiny is intended to provide information required to evaluate the advantages and risks involved in the proposed transaction. As cited above, due diligence is more than merely analyzing past and prospective financial statements and is required to begin with a systematic assessment of the strategic logic and conclude with a statement relating to the investors' ability to realize value from the proposed project. While structured as an independent investigation, due diligence could also help uncover hitherto overlooked good news.

The due diligence process is an objective assessment of the business case in its entirety and essentially involves questioning and validating each assumption – major or minor, (Cullinan, Le Roux and Weddigen, 2004).

While project proponents could be swayed by technical details, project analysts are required to adopt a disciplined approach and view the project from a distance to confirm the viability of the business proposition.

The process encompasses a view of the business environment in the proposed country or region, the industry and regulations affecting it and finally the value chain of which the proposed project would form a part. Elaborate discussions with proposed customers, especially in the case of power generation projects where the electricity utility is likely to be the sole customer — a market condition economists refer to as 'monopsony', or with airline companies in the case of airport projects would be a vital first step. Among other things, it is essential to establish the solvency and liquidity of the customers to ensure that payments for the services delivered are received in a timely manner.

Competition for the services delivered by the proposed project could emanate from either within the industry or from potential substitutes, as for example, with alternative modes of transportation or with certain types of reinforced plastics replacing metals. A comprehensive analysis of the competitive scenario helps establish present and potent threats to the proposed project. Equipped with this background information, investors can explore the cost and other advantages from the proposed project, and the sustainability of such advantages, to counter existing and expected competition. Such due diligence examination could also enable the proponents develop innovative approaches or management structures to deliver the product or service at a lower cost.

A very significant contribution of such an investigation would be the potential synergies with existing projects, especially to counter cyclical or seasonal patterns. Alternatively, a systematic analysis could also highlight potential conflicts with other projects, through cannibalization of market share and revenue erosion, for instance. Identifying these and other risks and deciding on the most appropriate mitigation measures that could be put in place at least-aggregate-cost to the project, is a key deliverable for the due diligence study.

Project analysts routinely undertake sensitivity and scenario analyses to analyze risk profiles of projects. Sensitivity analysis refers to changing the value of a single variable, holding all other input parameters constant, to test its impact on the eventual outcome viz., the investors' return on investment. It is employed to identify the variable(s) to which the given project is most sensitive. Analysts then recommend appropriate management measures to sustain the most desirable states of such variables. While all projects are impacted by the cost of financing, indirect expenses on regulatory compliance, taxation etc., flow type projects, could, for instance, be most sensitive to traffic volumes and the unit prices while mining projects could be intensely impacted by prevailing prices of the extracted material.

The financial model is drawn up with reasonable and foreseeable input parameters, commonly referred to as the 'base case' estimation of the project. A scenario analysis involves effecting a simultaneous change to the values of several variables to help the project proponent determine the best and worst states of the world. Suitable mitigation measures are then instituted to counter the relatively less desirable situations.

References

Banerjee, Sudeshna Ghosh. Oetzel, Jennifer M and Ranganathan, Rupe, Private Provision of Infrastructure in Emerging Markets: Do Institutions Matter?, *Development Policy Review*, Vol 24, Issue 2, 2006. p 175 – 202.

Cullinan, Geoffrey. Le Roux, Jean-Marc and Weddigen, Rolf-Magnus The Secrets of Great Due Diligence, Harvard Business School Working Knowledge, 3 May, 2004, hbswk.hbs.edu.

DeMott, John S, End of Six Year Ice Follies, *Time*, New York, 10 Nov, 1986.

Economist[a], The Face Value: Making the Trains Run on Time, The Economist Print Edition, 16th February, 2006.

Economist[b], The Economist Focus: The Great Unbundling, The Economist Print Edition, 18th January 2007.

Economist[c], The The Airbus A380: The Giant on the Runway, The Economist Print Edition, 11th October 2007.

Gomes, Francisco J. Kotlikoff, Laurence J and Viceira, Luis M. The Excess Burden of Government Indecision, Working Paper, National Bureau of Economic Research, 12 January, 2007.

Hill, Linda and Wetlaufer, Suzy Leadership When There is No One to Ask: An Interview With ENI's Franco Bernabe, Harvard Business Review, July – August 1998, p 81 – 94.

Lagace, Martha, Porsche's Risky Role on an SUV, Harvard Business School, Working Knowledge, http://hbswk.hbs.edu/item/5466.html, 5 September, 2006.

Lopes MDS and Flavell R. Project Appraisal – A Framework To Assess Non-Financial Aspects of Projects During the Project Life Cycle, *International Journal of Project Management*, Vol 16, Issue 4, August 1998, p 223 – 233.

Morris, Sebastian Cost and Time Overruns in Public Sector Projects, Economic and Political Weekly, 24 November, 1990, Vol XXV, No. 47, p M154 – M168.

Reichardt, C L. Due Diligence Assessment of Non-Financial Risk: Prophylaxis for the Purchaser, *Resources Policy*, Vol 31, Issue 4, December 2006, p 193 – 203.

Singh, Boeing L and Kalidindi, Satyanarayana N. Traffic Revenue Risk Management Through Annuity Model of PPP Road Projects in India, *International Journal of Project Management*, Vol 24, Issue 7, 2006 p 605 – 613.

Suxun and Chenjunnan Private Capital: What Impedes Its Entry Into China's Minerals Industry, Resources Policy, Vol 33, 2008, p 23 – 28.

Trump, Donald J. and Schwartz, Tony, The Art of the Deal, Ballantine Books, New York, 1987, p 301.

USA Today, 26 March, 2008, http://www.usatoday.com/travel/flights/2008-03-26-a380-ground_N.htm.

Vilanova, Laurent Financial Distress, Lender Passivity and Project Finance: The Case of Eurotunnel, Working paper, September 2006, http://ssrn.com/abstract=675304.

Annexure to Chapter 2

Ten commandments for non-financial risk assessment during due diligence†:

1. Accept that assessment of non-financial risk issues is an integral part of due diligence assessment.

2. Do not leave it until the 11th hour to address issues of non-financial risk—often these issues are complex and require a long lead time.

3. Integrate staff with the right mix of skills and experience to address non-financial risk into the due diligence team.

4. Make sure that there are no gaps between areas of assessment (or, conversely, no areas of excessive overlap), and employ lateral thinkers who will be able to reach beyond their own cultural setting and operational paradigm.

5. Where necessary, hire appropriately skilled and experienced consultants to supplement the due diligence team and treat them as part of the team.

6. Make sure that the person managing the due diligence process understands the significance of non-financial risk and is willing to stand by the findings of his team, even in the face of senior management pressure to press ahead with the acquisition.

7. Within the constraints of the time frame, seek out all pertinent information (both public and internal) and do not just rely on obvious sources.

8. Ground truth 'desk top' assessments with site visits wherever possible.

9. If the project is acquired, follow through on the due diligence findings and recommendations.

10. Develop a series of internal checklists and 'no go' activities for due diligence purposes and revise these for thoroughness and user friendliness in the light of completed due diligence assessments.

† Extract from Reichardt (2006)

Financial Modeling

KEY CHAPTER CONCEPTS

1. A capital investment decision is a resource allocation decision and the economic unit of account is cash.

2. Cash-flow modeling is used to confirm the project's ability to service its debt and to assess the availability of post-tax surpluses for distribution among equity investors.

3. A project is chosen for implementation when the rate of return generated is greater than the cost of capital applied.

4. The economic viability of a project can be affected by special tax considerations, such as the use of accelerated depreciation methods or the availability of tax holidays.

GLOSSARY OF NEW TERMS

Amortization payment of debt in a series of installments.

Bankable Project a stable enough project to ensure profitability and hence acceptable for processing by a bank.

Counter-factual scenario the scenario that would have been observed had the given event not materialized

Depreciation The systematic allocation of the first cost of an asset over its expected useful life.

DSCR Debt Service Coverage Ratio = EBITDA/debt service; measures the project's ability to service its debt.

Elasticity of Demand relationship between changes in quantity demanded of a good and changes in its price.

Net Cashflow Cash inflow minus cash outflow.

Normal Project or 'conventional' project, a project requiring an initial outlay of funds which is followed by a series of positive net cash inflows.

Opportunity cost value of the option foregone.

Sunk cost outlay already made or committed to be made.

Taking its Toll: Financial Modeling

The Noida Toll Bridge Company Limited[*] is a limited liability public company, specially constituted to build, own, operate and eventually transfer to the public agency concerned, the Delhi – Noida DND flyway, linking populations on either side of the River Yamuna which cuts through the National Capital Region of Delhi. The flyway was commissioned in February, 2001, slated to derive revenues from carrying traffic over the eight-lane trans-river link and the approach roads, and from the sale of advertising space on the route. The business proposition rests on the expectation that traffic from south Delhi to the satellite city of Noida and vice-versa would prefer to traverse the more comfortable route, despite the toll charges, as most alternate routes have been congested. Concurrent with a traffic growth of about 15% in the April–June quarter of 2007, the company hiked the toll collected from commuters[†].

The picture has not always been as rosy, though. When the flyway was opened for the public in early 2000, the company received a serious setback in the face of commuters' reluctance to pay for a service that was, up to that point in time, free of cost. Revenues for the first year of operations were, consequently, a mere 25% of original projections,

---

[*]   *www.ntbcl.com*
[†]   *Economic Times (2007)*

(*Continued*)

rising to about 29% in the second year. More remarkably, the number of paying commuters in the first year was 22,383 against an expected 97,068 and 38,465 against 103,835 in the second.

The situation has progressively improved for the toll bridge company and traffic volumes average upwards of 70,000 vehicles a day, (Zadoo, 2006), against the flyway capacity of 200,000 vehicles per day. That the toll and the operation and maintenance expenditure are linked to prevailing inflation has also worked in favor of the company.

A toll road like the DND Flyway lends itself to an interesting study in project appraisal and investment. The revenue model for the project would be relatively straightforward to construct, with two sources, namely the toll and earnings from advertising. The operation and maintenance expenses are readily recognizable: paid to the contractor either as a fixed amount or as a percentage of revenues. Demand for the service is presumed to remain stable, irrespective of the price payable. This is unrealistic. Use of the toll road, as it turns out, actually declines with rising prices, and the project planners have obviously ignored the elasticity of such demand. Under these circumstances, a retroactive financial model, incorporating actual traffic volumes and revenues, indicating that the company would require over five years to record its maiden profit would clearly not reflect a bankable project. A robust financial model accounts for such variability in demand corresponding to a range of price points and a sensitivity analysis helps optimize project size and pricing.

Introduction

The purchase and installation of new equipment, acquiring real estate or building, developing a new product or setting up a new manufactory, the implementation of an infrastructure project, or acquiring concessions for oil exploration are examples of projects requiring significant initial outlays, potentially yielding returns over a prolonged time horizon. Further, it is nearly impossible to revisit the investment mid-way and a reversal often entails substantial additional expenditure.

This is more so the case with stand-alone independent projects with highly specific assets, such as the Eurotunnel discussed in the last chapter. The preparation of a financial model, containing, among other things, the cash-flow projections is a critical part of the analysis and investment decision-making process. The cash-flow streams associated with any project fall into three broad categories: (i) initial investment or project cost, (ii) operating cash-flows and (iii) terminal value or salvage value. Even as strategic concerns and market power assessments drive strategic decision-making, actual investments are driven by cash-flow considerations. In the case of standalone projects, the estimation of cash-flows is relatively straightforward. However, in the case of firms implementing a portfolio of projects, the viability of each project needs to be established in isolation. The addition of a project to the existing lot is decided on the basis of the incremental cash-flows: the cash-flow evolution with the project minus the cash-flow that would have materialized had the project not been taken up (counter-factual scenario).

Project Cost: Fixed and Working Capital

The project cost comprises the capital expenditure on engineering, land, building, labor, construction, the landed cost of equipment and the fees paid to designers, consultants, lawyers etc. Generally, the interest payable on debt, during the tenure of project construction, is mentioned separately but, for the purpose of the financial analysis, is considered an integral part of the upfront cost of the project. Preliminary, pre-incorporation and pre-operative expenses associated with having the project company registered and operations set-up are part of the upfront costs. Subsidies and grants received from governments or donor agencies are deducted from the project's upfront costs. Financial guarantees, security deposits etc. which overlap with the tenure of the project are considered a part of the first cost and their eventual recovery is recorded alongside the terminal value realized from the project. By definition, projects in operation do not call for large periodic investments or maintenance expenditure and hence enjoy surplus free cash-flows, thus doing away with the need for infusion of working capital from external sources such as banks. Working capital necessary for smooth operations of the project is generally miniscule in comparison with the capital expenditure and is generally met out of the project revenues.

Operating cash-flows are computed by adding back the depreciation and other non-cash charges to the earnings after tax. Of this, the cash-outflows such as the repayment of debt are deducted to compute the cash available for distribution among the shareholders.

The terminal cash-flows include the post-tax proceeds from the sale of capital assets, salvage value of project assets and other receipts. As mentioned above, the recovery of margin money left with banks, security deposits and other elements of working capital are added back to the cash-on-hand. Obviously, the more distant cash inflows, such as salvage value of equipment, are more difficult to predict. The return benchmarks for the project should provide for such uncertainty.

A few basic principles should be applied during the estimation of project cash-flows including the following:

- Include only incremental cash-flows: the impact of the project on the cash-flow stream should be gauged after eliminating expenses that would be incurred independent of the project's implementation, viz., head office costs.

- Ignore Sunk Costs: A sunk cost: is a commitment made or an expenditure already incurred. Such outflow is not linked to the decision relating to the project's eventual implementation. The professional fee paid for the conduct of an environmental and social impact assessment of a proposed project, for example, cannot be recovered and hence such expenditure should not influence the go / no-go decision. The only relevant costs are the incremental outlays proposed to be made if the project is undertaken and the penalties and other charges payable if the project is not undertaken.

- Ignore writing down allowances and other non-cash charges: the depreciation of the project assets as recorded in the books of account is a non-cash charge i.e., such write-downs do not involve actual cash transactions for the project and hence should be excluded from an analysis of the cash-flows.

- Cash-flows should be measured on an after-tax basis: the dividends accruing to equity holders are paid from post-tax profits and in this context, tax could be considered analogous to an expense made by the project company.

- The opportunity cost of resources employed should be included if project implementation involves the diversion of men or material from alternative applications, the consequent loss in revenue, if any, should be considered a cost to be borne by the project.

The Financial Model

The financial model of a project is acutely dependent on the reliability of the inputs and assumptions to provide requisite comfort to prospective lenders and investors. The first step in laying out a detailed financial model is the preparation of the profit and loss account (also referred to as the income statement). Projects generally have few — often in the order of three - sources of revenue from delivering services. In the case of the DND flyway discussed at the beginning of this chapter, the two sources of revenue are the toll paid by commuters using the roadway and sale of advertising space along the route. Preparation of the revenue model entails the estimation of traffic volumes and the evolution of toll charges over the life of the project. Similarly, the area available for sale to advertisers and the revenue expected per unit area are estimated.

In order to illustrate the preparation of a detailed financial model, we develop a model for the installation and operation of a wind energy generator (wind turbine). A wind turbine exhibits the typical characteristics of a project i.e., standalone asset, clearly discernable cash-flows, large upfront capital expense and minimal operational outlays and a small terminal value. Schmitz (2008) observes that wind energy developments qualify for project financing alongside any conventional large energy project. Such financing comes as a combination of debt and equity, optimized to suit the risk profile of the project and aligned with the expected cash-flow patterns. The most obvious risks in the acquisition of a wind turbine relate to the technology, wind resource availability and the off-take agreements for the power produced. The technology risks relating to the reliability and availability of service and spare components, has attained a generally acceptable standard and lenders are comfortable with the technology and with the manufacturers. The manufacturers are generally considered financially sound to fulfill their commitments under warranty and post-installation service agreements. The useful life of a wind turbine is estimated to be 20 years.

Wind farm developers study wind resource patterns at the proposed site for many years prior to installing the turbines. This, combined with general meteorological data, gives investors and lenders the requisite confidence. Additionally, the operation and maintenance contracts are stringent and binding to ensure that the available resource is completely harnessed. It is also possible for the project proponent to transfer the resource risk to either the maintenance contractor, through an appropriately structured contract or by procuring an insurance cover for the purpose. Connecting the wind turbines to the utility grids to transmit the power generated could be a cause for concern. Investors need to be convinced of the capacity of the transmission infrastructure to take on the additional power generated. More importantly, the solvency of the power consumer is a vital consideration to ensure that payments for the power supplied are received promptly.

Having evaluated the strategic aspects of the project, namely the availability of the resource, the conversion technology, the logistics and the market for the output from such conversion – the power generated – we go on to develop a financial model to evaluate the financial returns on the acquisition of a wind turbine.

Revenue Model

The revenue model, in this case, consists of the power generated and sold at the applicable tariff payable by the power consumer. To keep things simple, we consider that the power is wheeled to the electric utility itself. The financial model being constructed should reflect the viability or otherwise of the project, given the expected power output and the tariff payable. The tariffs are generally fixed, escalated by a certain margin each year or indexed to a standard inflation measure. Investors and lenders take comfort from predictable and stable revenue streams from fixed or steadily rising tariffs. Electricity revenues can be predicted with accuracy, primarily because the 'market' for electricity is assumed to be perpetual, while the tariffs are defined through the off-take agreements and the quantity of electricity generated by a given generator is pre-defined. The revenue model for a single 1.5MW capacity wind turbine, costing Indian Rupee ten crore (INR 100 million) would be constructed in Table 3.1:

Table 3.1: Input parameters for Revenue Model

Project Revenues (Input parameters)		
Annual power generation	lakh kWh	45
Rate per unit sold	INR	3.2
Annual escalation	%	0

Given no escalation in power tariffs, the revenue from the sale of power generated, remains constant at INR 1.44 crore (INR 14.4 million), for the plan horizon. However, if the utility executes a power off-take agreement which includes a 2% escalation in tariff per annum, the revenue stream for the first seven years is in Table 3.2:

Table 3.2: Projected Revenue Model with 2% Annual Escalation in Power Tariff

Year	1	2	3	4	5	6	7
Revenue from sale of power	144.00	146.88	149.82	152.81	155.87	158.99	162.17

We then go on to estimate the outflows on the upkeep and operation of the wind turbine. A maintenance contract is executed with a qualified agency with a promise to pay INR 15 lakh (INR 1.5 million) from year 2, with an annual escalation of 10%. An insurance policy is procured at the cost of INR 1 lakh (INR 0.1 million) per annum, assumed to remain constant over the life of the asset, to protect the project against resource and technology risks, and against earthquakes and other such perils. We have now arrived at a stage where the total revenues and the total expenditure are estimated, enabling us to compute the earnings before interest, tax and depreciation (EBITDA) as in Table 3.3.

Table 3.3: Projected EBITDA Values

Year	1	2	3	4	5	6	7
REVENUES							
Revenue from sale of power	144.00	146.88	149.82	152.81	155.87	158.99	162.17
EXPENSES							
O&M Expenses	0.00	15.00	16.50	18.15	19.97	21.96	24.16
Insurance Expenses	1.00	1.00	1.00	1.00	1.00	1.00	1.00
Total Expenses	1.00	16.00	17.50	19.15	20.97	22.96	25.16
EBITDA	143.00	130.88	132.32	133.66	134.91	136.03	137.01

Debt Capacity and Loan Amortization

The project's capital structure — the relative proportions of debt and equity in the initial outlay is determined by analyzing the profitability and the timing of cash-flows for the project. We commence with an initial assumption of the capital structure, say, 50% each or a ratio of 1:1. We use this preliminary structure to compute the interest charge on the project. In a circular computation, the project's liquidity in-turn feeds into the redesign of the capital structure. We revisit the ratio and align it with the project's ability to service such debt. This is easily accomplished with modern-day spreadsheet software. In essence, project sponsors prefer to maximize the leverage subject to the lender's comfort levels and to the project's ability to service such debt. Capital structure optimization is discussed in the next chapter.

The loan amortization schedule helps compute the debt service due from the project for each of the years covering the tenure of the debt. For the purpose of illustration, we consider a ten-year loan and assume that the principal is repaid in equal installments. The interest charge on the outstanding loan, for any given year, depends on the frequency of payments viz., annual, semi-annual, quarterly, monthly etc.

Table 3.4 contains the preliminary loan amortization schedule. The project begins with a loan of INR 500 lakh (INR 50 million) and repays the principal at INR 50 lakh each year for 10 years. The principal out-standing at the end of each year is the initial amount less the principal repaid during the year. To serve as a rough estimate, the interest charge is computed by averaging the principal outstanding for the year – the arithmetic mean of the outstanding principal at the beginning and the end of the respective year. The interest charge is the product of the interest rate on the loan, assumed 11% in this case, and the average outstanding principal. This interest charge is transferred to the profit and loss account.

The quantum of debt is then revisited and adjusted to match the project's ability to sustain such debt service. The amortization schedule is redrawn and the process is repeated with the computation spread out to match the repayment frequency stipulated in the loan agreement viz., a semi-annual loan repayment schedule would comprise twenty install-ments for the repayment of the principal with corresponding interest computations. The financial model is made available with this book at www.verdurous.in.

Table 3.5 illustrates the computation of the debt service coverage ratios (DSCR = EBITDA / debt service due) intended to convince lenders on the project's ability to repay the principal and interest on the debt.

Table 3.4: Loan Amortization Schedule

Year	1	2	3	4	5	6	7	8	9	10
Loan at year beginning	500	450	400	350	300	250	200	150	100	50
Repaid during year	50	50	50	50	50	50	50	50	50	50
Loan at year end	450	400	350	300	250	200	150	100	50	0
Average o/s loan	475	425	375	325	275	225	175	125	75	25
Interest	52.2500	46.7500	41.2500	35.7500	30.2500	24.7500	19.2500	13.7500	8.2500	2.7500

Table 3.5: Computation of Debt Service Coverage Ratios

Year	1	2	3	4	5	6	7	8	9	10
Principal payment	50	50	50	50	50	50	50	50	50	50
Interest payment	52.25	46.75	41.25	35.75	30.25	24.75	19.25	13.75	8.25	2.75
Total debt service	102.25	96.75	91.25	85.75	80.25	74.75	69.25	63.75	58.25	52.75
EBITDA	143.00	130.88	132.32	133.66	134.91	136.03	137.01	137.84	138.49	138.94
DSCR	1.39853	1.35276	1.45005	1.55876	1.68106	1.81974	1.9784	2.16215	2.3774	2.63392

Average	1.84129
Minimum	1.35276

In situations where equipment or real estate is leased, imposing a periodic rental charge on the project, the ratio is computed to ensure coverage of such fixed charge for the contracted tenure. DSCR values greater than 1.0 confirm that the project generates sufficient cash (EBITDA) in the given year to repay the principal, interest and other contracted liabilities due in that year. Lenders are generally concerned with the values of the ratios during the nascent stages of the project, pending stabilization of operations and hence are known to insist on certain minimal values, of the order of 1.5 or 2.0, commensurate with the risk profile and of the project.

Depreciation of Assets

Depreciation is the systematic allocation of the first cost of the project assets over their useful life or as specified by the applicable accounting standard. The annual depreciation is an entry in the books of account and does not involve an actual cash outlay. It is intended to reflect the wear down of the project asset, consequent to routine use. By the same token, land is not depreciated on the books of account to remain consistent with real world situations where land seldom wears down or loses value owing to routine usage. We spread the depreciation of the wind turbine asset (excluding the cost of land estimated at INR 1.8 million) over the estimated twenty year life.

Taxation

The earnings after tax (EAT) are computed by deducting the tax payable from the earnings before tax but after allowing for the interest charge and the depreciation on the assets. In the accounting periods where the earnings before tax are negative, the losses are carried forward to subsequent periods and netted against profits earned in those periods, in keeping with prevailing statutory mandates. The tax payable is then computed on the net earnings.

Table 3.6 displays the profit and loss account, for the first 10 years, for the proposed wind turbine installation. Profits earned in those periods are in accordance with the prevailing statutory mandates.

Table 3.6: Projected Profit and Loss Account

Year	1	2	3	4	5	6	7	8	9	10
Revenue from sale of power	144.00	146.88	149.82	152.81	155.87	158.99	162.17	165.41	168.72	172.09
O&M Expenses	0.00	15.00	16.50	18.15	19.97	21.96	24.16	26.57	29.23	32.15
Insurance Expenses	1.00	1.00	1.00	1.00	1.00	1.00	1.00	1.00	1.00	1.00
Total Expenses	1.00	16.00	17.50	19.15	20.97	22.96	25.16	27.57	30.23	33.15
EBITDA	143.00	130.88	132.32	133.66	134.91	136.03	137.01	137.84	138.49	138.94
Interest Expenses	52.250	46.75	41.25	35.75	30.25	24.75	19.25	13.75	8.25	2.75
Depreciation	49.100	49.100	49.100	49.100	49.100	49.100	49.100	49.100	49.100	49.100
Earnings Before Tax (EBT)	41.65	35.03	41.97	48.81	55.56	62.18	68.66	74.99	81.14	87.09
Loss brought forward	0.0000	0.0000	0.0000	0.0000	0.0000	0.0000	0.0000	0.0000	0.0000	0.0000
PBT	41.6500	35.0300	41.9676	48.8140	55.5552	62.1761	68.6597	74.9873	81.1382	87.0895
Loss c/f	0.0000	0.0000	0.0000	0.0000	0.0000	0.0000	0.0000	0.0000	0.0000	0.0000
Taxable Profit	41.6500	35.0300	41.9676	48.8140	55.5552	62.1761	68.6597	74.9873	81.1382	87.0895
Tax	14.0236	11.7946	14.1305	16.4357	18.7054	20.9347	23.1177	25.2482	27.3192	29.3230
Earnings After Tax (EAT)	27.6264	23.2354	27.8371	32.3783	36.8498	41.2414	45.5420	49.7391	53.8190	57.7665

Statement of Cash Flows

The Profit and Loss Account drawn up above, conforms to accounting principles but does not necessarily reflect changes in the project's cash holding, largely owing to the recording of depreciation which is a non-cash charge and, the need for repayment of principal amounts against outstanding debt. Further, some of the income say from the sale of power to the electricity utility, while recognized as revenues in a particular accounting period on the basis of accruals, could materialise in subsequent accounting periods. Conversely, payments against recorded expenses could be actually made with a lag.

The statement of cash-flows provides relevant information about the project's cash receipts and cash payments during a particular accounting period. The document provides aggregate data regarding all cash inflows a project receives from routine operations, including interest earned on short-term cash deposits, as well as cash outflows that pay for project operations and upkeep. We progress the discussion on the wind turbine asset to illustrate the preparation of the statement of cash-flows. Table 3.7 presents the statement of cash-flows, for the first ten years, for the proposed wind turbine installation.

Drawing up the cash-flow statement is a significant milestone in the project preparation phase. It enables sponsors evaluate returns on their investments, while confirming the project's ability to service its debt commitments. The statement is subject to rigorous scrutiny to determine the best and worst case scenarios to help project sponsors put in place appropriate mitigation measures for the less preferred scenarios.

Balance Sheet

The balance sheet is a statement representing the financial position of the project at a given date, intended to update sponsors and lenders of

Table 3.7: Projected Statement of Cash-flows

Year	1	2	3	4	5	6	7	8	9	10
Earnings After Tax (EAT) from Profit & Loss Account		27.6264	23.2354	27.8371	32.3783	36.8498	41.2414	45.5420	49.7391	53.8190	57.7665
Add back depreciation	49.1000	49.1000	49.1000	49.1000	49.1000	49.1000	49.1000	49.1000	49.1000	49.1000
Cash inflow after tax, before depreciation	76.73	72.34	76.94	81.48	85.95	90.34	94.64	98.84	102.92	106.87
Principal repayment	−50	−50	−50	−50	−50	−50	−50	−50	−50	−50
Net cash-flow from project	26.73	22.34	26.94	31.48	35.95	40.34	44.64	48.84	52.92	56.87

the project's financial stability. The balance sheet carries information relating to the sources of project funding viz., sponsor equity and long-term debt and the assets acquired by applying such funding.

The balance sheet contained in Table 3.8 presents the financial position, for the first ten years, reflecting *inter alia*, the gradual repayment of long-term debt, the wear down of the project asset created and the accretion to reserves. The share capital remains at INR 500 lakh (INR 50 million), in keeping with the initial capital structure assumptions. The long-term debt is repaid over ten years, as shown in the amortization schedule in Table 3.4 above. The earnings after tax (EAT) from the Profit and Loss Account, in Table 3.6 above, are transferred to the reserve account and cumulated assuming that no dividends are paid to shareholders in the interim.

The total assets are computed from the cash on hand from the cash-flow statement from Table 3.7 above and the fixed assets, net of depreciation applied. Since the wind turbine is depreciated over a twenty year period, the initial book-value of the land attached to it shows up as the residual value of the assets at the end of the twenty year period. If the project is completely liquidated at the end of twenty years, the piece of land would be sold off at the prevailing market price and the applicable taxes paid on the earnings so derived.

The balance sheet provides the residual book-value of the project's assets at any point in time and thus helps arrive at interim valuations in case a change in ownership is contemplated. It also provides a tracking mechanism to confirm that the project has been disciplined in servicing outstanding debt. If an existing project is to be expanded, say, the addition of a couple of lanes to an existing toll road, the incremental investment should be weighed against the incremental cash-flows emanating from the expansion, as if it were a separate project. The balance sheet for the consolidated project would reflect such additions in assets and corresponding changes in funding patterns.

Table 3.8: Projected Balance Sheet

Year	1	2	3	4	5	6	7	8	9	10
Liabilities										
Share Capital	500	500	500	500	500	500	500	500	500	500
Long term debt	450	400	350	300	250	200	150	100	50	0
Reserves	27.63	23.24	27.84	32.38	36.85	41.24	45.54	49.74	53.82	57.77
Cumulative reserves	27.63	50.86	78.70	111.08	147.93	189.17	234.71	284.45	338.27	396.03
Total Liabilities	977.63	950.86	928.70	911.08	897.93	889.17	884.71	884.45	888.27	896.03
Assets										
Gross Fixed Assets	1000	950.9	901.8	852.7	803.6	754.5	705.4	656.3	607.2	558.1
Depreciation for the year	49.1	49.1	49.1	49.1	49.1	49.1	49.1	49.1	49.1	49.1
Net Fixed Assets	950.9	901.8	852.7	803.6	754.5	705.4	656.3	607.2	558.1	509
Cash and Bank balance	26.73	22.34	26.94	31.48	35.95	40.34	44.64	48.84	52.92	56.87
Cumulative cash balance	26.73	49.06	76.00	107.48	143.43	183.77	228.41	277.25	330.17	387.03
Total Assets	977.63	950.86	928.70	911.08	897.93	889.17	884.71	884.45	888.27	896.03
Difference check	0.00	0.00	0.00	0.00	0.00	0.00	0.00	0.00	0.00	0.00

Real Versus Nominal Valuations

A project analyst has to choose between preparing the financial model in nominal units and constant "real" units of currency i.e. by removing the effect of inflation. Cash-flow projections which involve escalating revenue items at a certain rate and expenditure items at a different rate would need to be substantiated. For instance, the escalation in revenue could be governed by long-term offtake contracts, not linked to prevailing inflation, while expenditure on operations could remain exposed to market conditions.

Generally, when a project's costs are denominated in a single currency, and the inflation expectations in the medium-term are reasonably anchored, it would be simpler to specify inflation assumptions and conduct a sensitivity analysis to evaluate various scenarios. Tham and Velez – Pareja (2001) go on to argue that investment appraisal based on financial statements with real values could be potentially misleading and that contemporary financial analysis with explicit mention of inflation expectations help minimise errors of omission. The analyst should also be cognizant that the financial model and other project documents are examined by professionals from diverse backgrounds viz., lawyers, bankers, consultants, etc., who would find it relatively straightforward to visualise actual amounts of cash involved in transactions. Further, interest rates on loans and investor return expectations are modeled in nominal terms and implicitly provide for respective inflation expectations.

Conclusion

A financial model is an *ex-ante* representation of the project's statements of account and is useful in demonstrating the project's ability to generate a respectable return on sponsors' investments while promptly servicing the debt availed. Prospective lenders and investors subject the financial model to rigorous scrutiny and validate each assumption prior to committing cash to the project. A robust financial model enables thorough sensitivity and scenario analyses to ascertain the vulnerability of the project to drastic changes in input variables.

References

Economic Times, 8 October, 2007, http://economictimes.indiatimes.com/article-show/2438168.cms

Schmitz, Stefan "Project Financing for Wind: Pointers and Pitfalls", 17 April, 2008, www.renewableenergyworld.com/rea/news/reworld/story?id=52028

Tham, Joseph and Velez-Pareja, Ignacio, "Modeling the Impacts of Inflation in Investment Appraisal", December 2001, http://ssrn.com/abstract=295060 or DOI: 10.2139/ssrn.295060

Zadoo, Vishaka "Corporate: The Rush Begins", Businessworld, 2006, http://www.businessworld.in/content/view/963/1018/

Optimization of Capital Structure

KEY CHAPTER CONCEPTS

1. Capital structure describes the relative quantum of debt and equity used to finance a project. By definition projects take on long-term debt and do not require short-term or permanent short-term (working capital) debt.

2. Project capital structure is driven by cash-flow patterns, debt capacity and lenders' mandates.

3. The project analyst is required to balance the lower cost of debt against the potential risk of illiquidity from servicing such contracted liabilities.

4. A project could start with a higher proportion of equity and subsequently, swap some of the equity for debt when cash inflows from operations stabilize.

GLOSSARY OF NEW TERMS

Capital Structure The sizing of long-term debt and equity used to finance a project.

Cost of Capital The rates of return demanded by the project's investors and lenders.

Mixed Capital Structure Funding drawn from long-term debt and equity used to finance a project as opposed to an all-equity funded project.

Pecking Order Preference sequence for financing: retained earnings, debt, convertible debt, common equity.

Pool of Funds Accumulation of capital from multiple sources for application to a particular investment project.

Tax Exhaustion the situation where the project does not have a large tax liability to benefit from the tax relief derived from high leverage.

Aborted Takeoff: Canary Wharf

The Reichmann brothers were scrupulously honest in their negotiating and had earned a reputation as people whose handshake was as good as a contract. Olympia & York Developments Limited (O&Y), their company, erected high-quality structures as scheduled and under budget, and progressively also came to be known for the innovative financing packages the brothers assembled. All of this earned them excellent working relationships with their tenants and the municipal and government officials with whom they came in contact.

The brothers burst onto the scene in the early 1970s when they announced the construction of the tallest building in Canada, the 3.5 million square feet, 72 storey office tower. This was followed by the acquisition of the Uris portfolio, a block of eight office buildings in Manhattan, which proved to be a phenomenal success. The Reichmanns next won the construction contract for the World Financial Center, a gigantic project comprising six buildings, adjacent to the World Trade Center in southern Manhattan.

In the late 1980s, O&Y initiated the development of the Canary Wharf* site in East London, an 83 acre site slated to be the largest

---

* *http://www.canarywharf.com/*

(*Continued*)

development project in the world and home to *One Canada Square*, Britain's tallest skyscraper. Unfortunately for the Reichmanns, in the early 1990s, the British economy entered a recession and the London commercial property market collapsed. The office space at Canary Wharf remained largely unoccupied and O&Y was rapidly turning illiquid as the contagion spread to other parts of the world. In May 1992, the company filed for bankruptcy, at which time it owed about US$ 20 billion to banks and investors.

The rapid erosion in O&Y's liquidity is attributed to the pyramid-like financing strategy that the Reichmann brothers had adopted. Each property was under a separate legal entity and the company's subsidiaries had raised debts against individual proper-ties, some of which was guaranteed by the parent, while others were secured by assets held by fellow subsidiaries. For example, the World Financial Center was funded with US$ 300m of equity and with debt borrowed below prime rate against the Uris properties. In the boom years of the 1980s, lenders contributed enormous sums and skyscrapers were constructed worldwide in unprecedented numbers. The glut left several properties unoccupied and depressed the market valuations of available real estate. O&Y, which had amassed huge debts found that its properties were now worth less than the debt it owed to the ninety-odd banks and other lenders[†].

In the twelve weeks to mid-May of 1992, the company had defaulted on US$1 billion payments that had fallen due. In New York City, where the company was the largest commercial landlord, paying 2% of the city's total property taxes, O&Y was in sight of defaulting on US$ 75 million in taxes payable in short order[‡]. Fortunately for O&Y, most of the financing on its New York properties was on project financing terms – without recourse to the parent company's other assets – and even as it was in danger of losing individual properties, one at a time, it hoped to keep the holding company intact. Eventually, creditors decided to

---

[†]   *Hylton (1992)*
[‡]   *Malkin (1992)*

(*Continued*)

restructure the debt payments in exchange for about 80 percent of the company's equity, effecting an equity-for-debt swap and deciding that O&Y equity was likely to be worth more when the market conditions improved, as against liquidating its properties in a deflationary market.

Introduction

The capital structure of a project describes the amount of long-term debt and equity – common and preferred - employed. While the capital structure remains constant for most projects, it is not uncommon, even advisable, to switch structures as cash-flow patterns stabilize.

This chapter discusses the significance of optimising a project's capital structure and illustrates the process through the wind turbine acquisition model from the previous chapter. Essentially, the optimal capital structure minimises the weighted cost of capital employed on the project, thus maximising shareholder value. While employing high leverage with its contingent low cost is obviously tempting, it has to be tempered with the risks of running out of free cash and into potential bankruptcy. The capital structure of a project affects the distribution of operating income among various constituents: debt holders with fixed periodic claims and equity holders with residual claims.

Background

The Modigliani and Miller "M & M" articles of 1958 and 1963 form the bedrock on which the edifice of literature pertaining to capital structure optimisation rests. The M & M *no tax* capital structure hypothesis identified circumstances in which capital structure could be irrelevant implying that the investment and financing decisions are independent.

The so called 'Irrelevance Proposition' is, of course, subject to stringent and very significant assumptions including:

- The project in question is not subject to taxation.

- The project faces no transaction costs.

- Access to information is cost-less.

- Bankruptcy is cost-less: if the company goes bankrupt, it is possible to liquidate its assets and distribute the proceeds among various claimants at no cost.

- Corporate bodies and Individuals could borrow at the same interest rates, which remain constant at various levels of leverage.

- Companies do not enjoy limited liability protection and are perceived to be as risky as individuals.

In the previous chapter, we have built the financial model, including the balance sheet, for a typical project, as the first step to making the investment decision and thereby working towards increasing shareholder wealth. The M & M proposition leads us to believe that the two halves of the balance sheet are independent of each other. In the real world, where the stringent assumptions are relaxed, capital structure does matter and the two halves of the balance sheet are not really independent. The synchronization between the financing and investment decisions is mandatory for project companies which are structured as special purpose vehicles with the express purpose of executing a given project. The mobilization of financial resources is therefore very obviously linked to the proposed investment.

Owing to the transparency in application of funds, project-specific companies typically take on a far greater proportion of debt, as compared to conventional multi-activity corporations listed on the world's stock exchanges. In a world with corporation taxes, higher leverage reduces the tax payable by the project company. Consequently, it is possible to optimise the use of debt and equity to fund a given project to maximise shareholder wealth. In other words, both, the project's investment and financing decisions could each influence shareholder wealth.

The effective cost of debt to the project in a world with taxation is given by:

$$K_D = (1 - T)(K_d)$$

Where K_D is the post-tax (effective) cost of debt, T is the applicable tax rate and K_d is the pre-tax (nominal) cost of debt.

In addition to lowering the tax charge on the project vehicle, higher leverage disciplines managers by compelling periodic payments to lenders in accordance with the loan amortization schedule. This provides an additional level of supervision on managers and addresses the commonly observed free cash-flow problem[†]. Systematic repayment of contracted liabilities and fixed charges prevents misallocation of the project's free cash.

Project debt is secured against the project assets and debt holders have the first claim on the project's free cash-flow. Higher leverage, clearly, imposes higher fixed liabilities on the project, which could suck the project dry of available liquidity, potentially even leading to the company's bankruptcy, as in the O & Y case outlined at the beginning of this chapter. Balancing the advantages of high leverage with the risks associated with illiquidity, especially at the early stages of a project, is the essence of the capital structure optimisation problem.

Weighted Cost of Capital

A mixed capital structure, comprising equity and debt in varying proportions is most common in practice. Shareholders make their investment decisions basing on minimum acceptable returns for the project, benchmarked against the opportunity cost of applying their capital. Similarly, debt capital faces a certain opportunity cost, identified with alternative projects with comparable risk profiles.

Financial resources thus mobilised are applied to the particular project and it flows that the cost of using funds out of this accumulated 'pool' is the weighted average of the individual inputs. The weighted

---

† *By definition, a project company does not face opportunities for investing internal accruals, even though it ranks high on managers' preferences.*

average cost of capital (WACC) from various sources is employed as the Net Present Value (NPV) discount rate, for a given capital structure (computation is demonstrated in subsequent chapters).

The weighted average cost of capital K_0 is given by:

$$K_0 = \frac{(V_E \times K_E) + (V_D \times K_D)}{(V_E + V_D)}$$

Where V_E, V_D are respectively, the values of equity and debt invested into the project and K_E, K_D are return expectations of shareholders and lenders.

Project Equity Investments

A project company is funded by equity capital from a small number of individual and institutional investors. While this could potentially limit the quantum of investment, it has several advantages. Separation of ownership and control which is the central characteristic of a joint stock corporation does not work in favor of project companies. A small number of owners could directly govern the project company and hence avoid the principal-agent problem. This also enables key project decisions that need to be made expeditiously, and facilitates aggressive negotiations with prospective lenders. The circulation of information is restricted and hence confidential data does not reach potentially adversarial entities.

Vilanova (2006) has categorically stated that "governance problems associated to dispersed equity ownership may be worse in project companies than in other less indebted firms". This is readily illustrated in the case of Eurotunnel, where the construction companies, who were some of the initial shareholders, designed contractual structures that were unfavorable to the operating company. When these promoter companies sold their shareholding and as ownership was transferred to large numbers of individual investors, Eurotunnel lacked the voice to defend its interests. This weakness was accentuated when the company eventually defaulted on its debt commitments and when the banks took control of the Eurotunnel board. The banks lacked the technical expertise required to mitigate the weaknesses in the contracts or to contest the contractors' claims.

Equity ranks lowest in the pecking order as a source of financing and holders are residual claimants on the free cash flow available with the project company (holders of preferred equity, as in conventional financing structures, are senior in claim only to the holders of common equity). It is also possible to cumulate preferred dividends if necessary. Equity holders, therefore, are predisposed to less predictable pay outs from project companies, especially in the early stages of operations. The project could, in certain states of the world, hold the potential for a significant upside for the owners, which would entice them to absorb the risk of such variability. Conversely, debt holders do not have a claim (except through specially constructed hybrid instruments) on the upside and hence would not be willing to absorb additional risk. Project companies such as O&Y Developments run aground because they apply greater amounts of debt against relatively modest amounts of equity, even prior to eliminating the volatility in cash flows. The equity for debt swap effected by lenders, as a part of the restructuring effort, is a mere rectification of this adverse situation.

Lender Stipulations and Constraints on Leverage

A typical project is highly leveraged. Hence, the major suppliers of finance i.e. the debt-holders, facing the classical principal-agent problem owing to the asymmetric availability of information in comparison with project 'insiders', choose to impose very restrictive covenants (conditions) on loan agreements, installing among other things, a process for periodic verification of the state of the project. In a world with imperfect information the net gains from information generation are substantial. Project financing with high leverage is beneficial as prospective lenders incur lower screening costs in evaluating a legally separate entity intending to undertake a discretely identifiable project, (Shah and Thakor, 1987).

Being at the head of the queue of claimants on the free cash-flow generated by the project, debt holders would require to be paid before dividends are distributed among shareholders. In order to ensure that project sponsors have enough 'skin in the game' to strive towards making the project work, debt holders typically impose certain threshold equity investment requirements as a precondition to providing debt, (Cullen, 2004).

As a company increases its level of debt, an increasing proportion of its free cash is periodically paid out as interest and towards other fixed charges. Despite the most rigorous scrutiny of the financial model, the cash-flows emanating from the operating project could vary in keeping with unprecedented market conditions. If the fixed charges are not adequately provided for, or if suitable insurance contracts are not put in place, to protect the project against such variability, there is a significant chance that the project's cash flow would be insufficient to meet the contracted payments. Sustained unavailability of free cash to meet such liabilities, for instance, during a recessionary environment, could lead lenders to force the project into bankruptcy.

A project benefits from the tax relief allowable on the interest payments (which is not available on dividends paid to shareholders). Tax exhaustion is a situation where the company does not face a large enough tax liability to be offset by the interest and other fixed charges due. The level of debt taken on by a project thus, is also determined by limits imposed by tax exhaustion, as debt capital loses its attraction as a tax shield, beyond this level.

Capital Structure Illustrated

We started with a 50% - 50% (1:1) debt – equity mix to model the wind turbine acquisition discussed in the previous chapter, yielding a series of debt service coverage ratios (DSCR) as laid out in Table 3.5 (Chapter 3). The lowest coverage ratio is encountered in year 2, progressively rising thereafter, for the tenure of the loan. We had assumed that the project could mobilize debt at 11%, pre-tax, which is equivalent to 7.30% after providing for the tax relief at a prevailing corporation tax rate of 33.67%. Assuming that the equity holders expect a threshold return of 20% on their investment into the project, the weighted average cost of capital for the wind turbine project is computed as in Table 4.1a:

Table 4.1a: Computation of Weighted Average Cost of Capital at 50:50 debt equity ratio

Source of Capital	Pre-tax Cost	Post-tax Cost	Proportion of Capital	Weighted Cost
Common Equity	20.00%	20.00%	50%	10.00%
Debt	11.00%	7.30%	50%	3.65%
			100%	13.65%

We simulate debt service coverage ratios for alternative capital structure scenarios and arrive at the optimal structure: in order of priority, ensuring availability of free cash to service the debt and minimising the cost of capital to the project. At 60% debt, the least coverage ratio is 1.127 (Table 4.2) and at 70% it falls below one to 0.966 (Table 4.3). By interpolation, the proportion of debt that ensures that the project achieves a DSCR of at least 1.0 lies between 70% and 60% - at 67.64% debt (and correspondingly, 32.36% equity). The Weighted Average cost of capital (WACC) at this capital structure, the lowest cost while the project is still able to meet its fixed (non-tax) commitments, is computed in Table 4.1b:

Table 4.1b: Computation of Weighted Average Cost of Capital at Least DSCR of 1.0

Source of Capital	Pre-tax Cost	Post-tax Cost	Proportion of Capital	Weighted Cost
Common Equity	20.00%	20.00%	32.36%	6.47%
Debt	11.00%	7.30%	67.64%	4.94%
			100%	11.41%

Table 4.1c: Computation of Weighted Average Cost of Capital at Least DSCR of 1.25

Source of Capital	Pre-tax Cost	Post-tax Cost	Proportion of Capital	Weighted Cost
Common Equity	20.00%	20.00%	45.85%	9.17%
Debt	11.00%	7.30%	54.15%	3.95%
			100%	13.12%

However, if the lenders were to seek additional comfort against potential variability in project cash inflows, and prescribe a threshold DSCR of 1.25 as a pre-condition to providing debt to the project, the capital structure and the consequent WACC would be as in Table 4.1c.

Compliant Capital Structure

Satellite-based communications service provider Iridium, promoted by US based telecom equipment major, Motorola mobilised equity and debt (some of which was guaranteed by the parent) based on the theory that "Iridium, once built, would resemble a utility with high margins, high fixed cost, and steady cash flows[‡]." Before the decade of the 1990s ran out, Iridium defaulted on its debt and filed for bankruptcy. Clearly, lower than anticipated demand for 'anytime anywhere' communication had left the company with insufficient cash to meet its contracted obligations. The situation with Olympia and York Developments, discussed at the beginning of this chapter, is identical. The company's properties had not yet been fully occupied and rentals had not stabilised. Consequently, when the debt service fell due, the company was cash-strapped.

Projects faced with construction or market uncertainties would be better served if they commenced with a relatively lower level of

---

[‡]   *Ho Kim et al. (2002)*

Table 4.2: Computation of DSCR for 60:40 Debt - Equity Ratio

Year	1	2	3	4	5	6	7	8	9	10
Principal payment	60	60	60	60	60	60	60	60	60	60
Interest payment	62.7	56.1	49.5	42.9	36.3	29.7	23.1	16.5	9.9	3.3
Total debt service	122.7	116.1	109.5	102.9	96.3	89.7	83.1	76.5	69.9	63.3
EBITDA	143.00	130.88	132.32	133.66	134.91	136.03	137.01	137.84	138.49	138.94
DSCR	1.16544	1.12730	1.2083	1.29896	1.40088	1.51645	1.64873	1.80179	1.98123	2.19493

Average	1.53441
Minimum	1.12730

Table 4.3: Computation of DSCR for 70:30 Debt - Equity Ratio

Year	1	2	3	4	5	6	7	8	9	10
Principal payment	70	70	70	70	70	70	70	70	70	70
Interest payment	73.15	65.45	57.75	50.05	42.35	34.65	26.95	19.25	11.55	3.85
Total debt service	143.15	135.45	127.75	120.05	112.35	104.65	96.95	89.25	81.55	73.85
EBITDA	143.00	130.88	132.32	133.66	134.91	136.03	137.01	137.84	138.49	138.94
DSCR	0.99895	0.96626	1.03575	1.11340	1.20075	1.2998	1.4132	1.54439	1.6982	1.88137

Average	1.31521
Minimum	0.96626

leverage and they subsequently took over more debt as operations stabilise. Classical examples include toll roads which take a few years for volumes to stabilise or stock-type projects which face exploration, reserve, access or price uncertainty. Such a modification of the capital structure could help reduce bankruptcy risks and simultaneously maximise shareholder wealth by lowering the cost of downstream debt - mobilised a few years into the project - as lenders perceive such debt as being less risky.

Capital Structure Optimization

Business risk is a significant factor in determining capital structure design. In general, it is recommended that the more stable and predictable the cash inflows from project operations, the greater the leverage effected and hence the lower the risk of bankruptcy. Conversely, the more volatile the cash earnings from the project, the higher the proportion of equity capital taken on by the project: the variability of sales volumes (traffic on toll roads), the variability in selling prices (commodities) or volatility in input costs (new product development) are better absorbed by a project with a lower leverage.

In the real world, projects often display characteristics which mandate a higher proportion of equity, especially at the early stages, and subsequently mature into 'utility-type' projects with inelastic demand patterns, capable of absorbing a greater quantum of debt. This switch between higher equity and higher leverage structures is relatively straightforward and is accomplished at lower cost by privately held project companies borrowing from banks, as compared to publicly listed corporations issuing fixed income securities. The financial model needs to be appropriately modified to reflect such changes in capital structure. The WACC is also revisited and the project's NPV computed for discrete time periods, discounted at the WACC applicable for each period. The consolidated NPV is then computed by the traditional method.

References

Cullen, Ann 'The Big Money for Big Projects: Interview with Benjamin Esty', Harvard Business School Working Knowledge, 14 June, 2004. http://hbswk.hbs.edu/item/4186.html

Ho Kim, Stephen In; Yoon Lee, Byung; Yong Park, Jai and Yong Ku, Tae, "Dominant Fit and Value Creation: Lessons From Nucor Revolution and Iridium Fiasco", Annual International Conference of the Strategic Management Society, 2002, http://bus.hanyang.ac.kr/dynamics/e_frame3_2002.htm

Hylton, Richard D. "Olympia and York's Properties are Valued Below its Debts", The New York Times, 18 May, 1992.

Malkin, Lawrence "A Debt Drama for the Decade: Olympia & York", The International Herald Tribune, 18 May, 1992.

Modigliani, Franco and Miller, Merton "The Cost of Capital, Corporation Finance and the Theory of Investment", American Economic Review, June 1958.

Modigliani, Franco and Miller, Merton "Corporation Income Taxes and the Cost of Capital", American Economic Review, June 1963.

Shah, Salman and Thakor Anjan V. "Optimal Capital Structure and Project Financing", Journal of Economic Theory, 42, 209 – 243, 1987.

Vilanova, Laurent "Financial Distress, Lender Passivity and Project Finance: The Case of Eurotunnel", Working paper, September 2006, http://ssrn.com/abstract=675304.

Assessment of Project Viability

KEY CHAPTER CONCEPTS

1. The future is difficult to predict. Weaker form of the Law of Iterated Knowledge: "to understand the future to the point of being able to predict it, you need to incorporate elements from this future itself [§]."

2. The payback period is a preliminary measure indicating the timing of cash generation, providing sponsors with the option to deploy it elsewhere.

3. The investment in a project is approved if the projected internal rate of return (IRR) is greater than the cost of capital.

4. The net present value (NPV) criterion and the IRR offer identical outcomes for stand-alone projects.

GLOSSARY OF NEW TERMS

Hurdle rate minimum return acceptable to potential investors.

Financial Closure legally binding commitment by investors to mobilize funding for a project.

Internal Rate of Return (IRR) the discount rate equating the present value of expected cash-flows to the project investment (NPV = 0).

Net Present Value (NPV) the present value of the stream of expected project cash-flows, less the net investment made.

Payback period time taken for the cumulative cash inflows to equal the net project investment.

Self-liquidating asset A project asset which pays for itself.

[§] *Taleb (2007)*

The Panama Canal: The Decision to Expand

The referrendum according approval for the expansion of the Panama Canal is hailed as the most significant Panamanian decision ever: "the foundation to build a better country". The expansion includes the provision of two new sets of locks, 40% longer and 60% wider than the existing ones: one each at the Pacific and Atlantic sides of the Canal. The project also proposes to widen and deepen the existing navigational channels in Gatun Lake and the deepening of the Culebra Cut[*]. The US$ 5.2b project is expected to be completed in 2014, exactly 100 years after the original canal was commissioned. The increased toll from ships using the canal is expected to pay for the expansion. The canal currently generates annual revenues of US$ 1.40 b, which planners expect would rise to US $6.0 b post-expansion[†].

The Panama Canal accounts for 5% of all world shipping, or about 14,000 vessels a year. Demand has progressively outstripped available capacity, with ships having to wait in queue to pass through. Some of the larger ships carrying oil, grain and other container cargo are presently unable to use the inter-oceanic canal. The Panama Canal Authority (ACP), which runs the canal had warned that if measures were not taken immediately, business would be lost to altenative shipping routes.

---

[*]   *http://www.pancanal.com/eng/expansion/index.html*
[†]   *Lacey (2006)*

(*Continued*)

Further, Panama's northern neighbour, Nicaragua has proposed to construct a canal between the Pacific and Atlantic oceans.

The proposal by the ACP‡ claims that doubling canal capacity will enhance operational efficiency, and provide economic benefits to Panamanians, thus improving the quality of their lives. Tolls charged are to be progressively ramped up, eventually being doubled over 20 years. The enlarged canal is slated to carry an additional 1250 million PCUMS tons (1 Panama Canal Universal Measurement System ton = 100 cubic feet of cargo space), during the first 11 years of operations through 2025, corresponding to an internal rate of return (IRR) of 12% on the investment made. ACP expects to recover investment costs in ten years while repaying debts of about US\$ 2.3b in eight years. The canal is also expected to contribute ever increasing amounts to the Panamanian treasury. Yet, the state is not expected to endorse or guarantee debts undertaken by ACP for the project's execution.

A major investment decision such as the proposed expansion of the Panama Canal requires a detailed analysis supported by accurate projections of each input parameter. Investors compare projected returns against respective benchmark expectations, largely determined by the opportunity cost of funds. In the given situation, the ACP projects an IRR of 12% over the first 11 years of project operation – the expansion project is viewed in isolation – with a payback period of less than ten years. Potential investors and lenders seek to validate such claims prior to making financial commitments to projects.

---

‡   *ACP (2006)*

Introduction

For a proposed project to achieve financial closure, investors and prospective lenders need to be convinced of its technical feasibility and financial viability. Confirming technical feasibility includes validating the strategic aspects of the project while providing comfort that construction can be completed as scheduled. The financial model is developed to demonstrate that the project would yield positive returns on investment, even under less preferred scenarios, while continuing to service its debt.

This chapter illustrates the investment decision, basing on the discounted cash-flow analysis and through the computation of various return-on-investment measures. The free cash-flow of a project represents the primary source of funds to service project debt and to provide a reasonable rate of return to the sponsors: a self-liquidating project asset. The objective of the evaluation process is to identify and undertake projects that would help enhance the sponsors' wealth i.e. positive net present value (NPV) projects. The quantum, timing and certainty of expected future cash-flows are evaluated in relation to the quantum of the initial investment. In addition, lenders evaluate the collateral value of assets mortgaged against the loan, weighed by the possibility of actually enforcing their security interests in the given context. Returns from alternative projects with similar risk profiles are compared and capital allocated among the most attractive opportunities.

Background

In chapter 3, we had estimated the after-tax cash-flows, involving *inter alia* eliminating the impact of non-cash charges such as depreciation, and providing for the repayment of principal amounts against project debt. If the project under consideration is a part of a cluster, the incremental cash-flows — the difference between the sponsor's cash flows with and without the project — are drawn up similarly. Sunk costs and costs that would be incurred irrespective of whether the project is undertaken, viz., head office costs are ignored.

Tax as a Cost of Doing Business

The future cash-flows are measured on an after-tax basis since corporate taxes represent one of the costs of doing business, akin to administrative expenses. Revenues and expenses are recorded on an accrual basis for the purposes of tax computation, even when the cash-flows materialize in subsequent accounting periods. Tax holidays announced by governments to encourage investments into certain categories of projects delay tax outflows, thereby increasing the attractiveness of such projects. Depreciation write-down allowances also play a significant part in determining the timing of tax loading on the project. Depreciation (as well as depletion and amortization) could be accelerated subject to special provisions in the tax code, thereby postponing cash outflows for the project. Under certain circumstances, such special provisions could render bankable, an otherwise unviable project.

The quantum of debt invested into the project determines the interest expense, which in-turn influences the tax load on the project. The capital structure, therefore, plays an important role in tax out flows. As we have seen earlier, the ability of the project to generate the cash flows to service such debt, i.e. the debt capacity, reciprocally, determines the quantum of debt.

Project Viability Assessments

Even as some of the input parameters are secured by firm contracts, we cannot overlook the fact that investment appraisal and decision making consist of numerous forecasts, estimates and pure guesses about the future states of the world[§]. Numerical techniques employed provide the decision maker with signals, helping make the investment decision. This is very significant, since, people from diverse cultural backgrounds could interpret identical numerical

---

[§]   *"It is tough to make predictions, especially about the future"* Yogi Berra, Baseball coach.

measures in substantially different ways. Ashta (2006) points out that psychological influences viz. myopia, outsiders' perceptions of oneself, fairness, agency problems, group decision-making and group think, optimism and pessimism, overconfidence or hubris, could interact to bias the eventual investment decision, ultimately impacting value creation. Further, the weights assigned to the numerical measure could also be industry specific. In banking for instance, the decision to install ATMs or to offer internet banking services is supported by discounted cash-flow analyses as well as qualitative considerations. Alternatively, in research and development (R&D) intensive and extractive industries such as pharmaceuticals, oil & gas etc., qualitative measures tend to dominate investment decision making. Valuation in the retail industry is found to correlate strongly with prevailing conditions in the real estate sector, and investments are driven by both tangible and intangible assets, (Akalu and Turner, 2001).

The financial viability assessment of the project is undertaken from two different perspectives: the *total investment* and the *equity* points of view. The two approaches allow the analyst to study the incentive structures of the lenders and the equity investors respectively, to partake in the project. The total investment perspective helps "determine the overall strength of the project", (Tham, 1999). In practical terms, the return computation from the equity holders' perspective offers a measure for comparison against the opportunity cost of capital sought to be invested in the given project.

We extend the discussion on the wind turbine acquisition to discuss the most commonly used measures, viz., the payback period, the NPV and the IRR.

Payback Period

The traditional, rather straightforward and rapid, assessment is the payback method, referring to how quickly the project 'pays back' the initial capital invested. Recall from Corporate Finance discussions that the payback method can provide a rule for comparing several mutually exclusive projects, ranked in terms of the speed of payback: the project with the fastest payback being most favored. It is generally employed to ascertain the timing of cash availability, for planned future deployment.

The simple method, though, suffers obvious weaknesses. Cash-flows materializing beyond the payback period are ignored, while considering such cash-flows could lead to a different conclusion. Most significantly, the payback method overlooks the time value of money and fails to distinguish between cash-flows occurring closer to the commissioning of the project and those from further afar.

We compute the payback period for the wind turbine acquisition, given a debt–equity ratio of 1:1. We observe that by adding back the debt service to compute the total cash generated by the project, the initial investment of the INR 1000 lakh is paid back 8.53 years – by linear interpolation between years 8 and 9 (Table 5.1). However, the equity investors have to wait for over ten years to recover their investment of INR 500 lakh (Table 5.2).

The Net Present Value Analysis

The Net Present Value (NPV) of the project is the difference between the net investment and the discounted value of the wealth it generates. The NPV is the present value of the after tax cash-flows, discounted at the weighted average cost of capital (WACC). Assuming, as we did in chapter 3 that debt is available to the project at 11% and the equity investors expect a return of 20%, the WACC is computed below:

After-tax cost of debt to the project	= (1 − 33.67%) * 11%
	= 7.30%
The equity investors' hurdle rate	= 20%
Proportion of debt and equity	= 1:1

Table 5.1: Computation of Project Payback for 50:50 Debt - Equity Ratio

Year	1	2	3	4	5	6	7	8	9	10
Earnings After Tax (EAT) from Profit & Loss Account	27.6264	23.2354	27.8371	32.3783	36.8498	41.2414	45.5420	49.7391	53.8190	57.7665
Add back depreciation	49.1000	49.1000	49.1000	49.1000	49.1000	49.1000	49.1000	49.1000	49.1000	49.1000
Cash inflow after tax, before depreciation	76.73	72.34	76.94	81.48	85.95	90.34	94.64	98.84	102.92	106.87
Principal repayment	-50	-50	-50	-50	-50	-50	-50	-50	-50	-50
Net cash-flow	26.73	22.34	26.94	31.48	35.95	40.34	44.64	48.84	52.92	56.87
Total Debt Service	102.25	96.75	91.25	85.75	80.25	74.75	69.25	63.75	58.25	52.75
Total Cash-flow From The Project	128.98	119.09	118.19	117.23	116.20	115.09	113.89	112.59	111.17	109.62
Cumulative Cash-flow	128.98	248.06	366.25	483.48	599.68	714.77	828.66	941.25	1052.42	1162.03

Table 5.2: Computation of Payback for Equity holders for 50:50 Debt - Equity Ratio

Year	1	2	3	4	5	6	7	8	9	10
Cash inflow after interest and tax, but before depreciation	76.73	72.34	76.94	81.48	85.95	90.34	94.64	98.84	102.92	106.87
Principal repayment	-50	-50	-50	-50	-50	-50	-50	-50	-50	-50
Net cash-flow	26.73	22.34	26.94	31.48	35.95	40.34	44.64	48.84	52.92	56.87
Cumulative Cash-flow	26.73	49.06	76.00	107.48	143.43	183.77	228.41	277.25	330.17	387.03

Weighted Average Cost of Capital (WACC) = 13.65%

$$NPV = \sum_{t=0}^{n} \frac{CF_t}{(1+r)^t}$$

$$NPV = -1000 + \sum_{t=1}^{n} \frac{CF_t}{(1+13.36\%)^t}$$

We discount the total project cash-flows, (for the twenty year life of the asset), from Table 5.1 above at the WACC to compute the NPV for the wind turbine acquisition. The NPV for the *total* cash-flow, considering the initial investment of INR 1000 lakh stands at INR -176.38. From the equity investors' perspective, the NPV for the INR 500 lakh investment, discounted at the 20% expectation, basing on the *net cash-flow* row in Table 5.1 above, is -233.36.

The Internal Rate of Return Analysis

The internal rate of return (IRR) for the project is the discount rate which makes the NPV zero. Investors choose to undertake the project if the projected IRR exceeds the cost of capital. The IRR method is preferred by practitioners, owing to its simplicity and intuitive appeal.

$$\sum_{t=0}^{n} \frac{CF_t}{(1+IRR)^t}$$

The IRR along the lines of the NPV computation above – for the project's post-tax cash-flows and for the equity holders – stand, respectively, at 10.10% and 10.08%.

Interpretation of Analyses and Decision Making

In the Panama Canal expansion case *discussed at the beginning of the chapter*, decision makers have concluded that an IRR of 12% over the first

11 years of canal operations would be the best use of the capital available. Further, a payback of just about ten years is considered reasonable, as the expanded canal is expected to have a much longer life time. The investment decision, therefore, has to be made in context.

1. The NPV and IRR rules point in the same direction. The wind turbine project comes up with negative values for the NPV, implying that implementation would take away from investors' wealth. The IRR, similarly, for the project as a whole is lower than the WACC. The IRR for the equity investors is only 10.08%, substantially lower than the 20% threshold expectation. In other words, if a potential investor had to choose between two mutually exclusive opportunities with identical risk profiles, one yielding the benchmark 20% and the other being the wind turbine under consideration, the investor would be better off with the alternative project.

2. The payback period for the wind turbine project, from the equity investors' perspective exceeds ten years. In other words, if a potential investor has plans for the redeployment of the funds, say, in five years, the cash would not be available for the purpose. An investor would choose to invest in the project if the payback period is found acceptable.

Sensitivity and scenario analyses are illustrated in the next chapter to assess the variables having the most significant impact on the viability of the project and to identify the most and least preferred future scenarios.

References

ACP "Proposal for the Expansion of the Panama Canal", Panama Canal Authority, 24 April, 2006 p 12 – 13.

Akalu, Mehari Mekonnen and Turner, Rodney "The Practise of Investment Appraisal: An Empirical Enquiry", Erasmus Research Institute of Management, The Netherlands, December 2001.

Ashta, Arvind, "Behavioral Influences on the Calculation of Expectations in Project Appraisal", Cahiers du CEREN 15 (2006) p 11 – 26.

Lacey Marc "Panamanians Vote Overwhelmingly to Expand Canal", New York Times, 23 October 2006.

Taleb, Nassim Nicholas (2007) The Black Swan, Allan Lane, UK p 172.

Tham, Joseph "Financial Discount Rates in Project Appraisal", Discussion Paper No. 706, Harvard Institute for International Development, Harvard University, 1999.

Analysis of Project Risk

KEY CHAPTER CONCEPTS

1. Potential investors evaluate macro or environmental risk and then drill down to project-specific risk.
2. Sensitivity analysis involves the identification of key variables potentially impacting project outcomes.
3. Scenario analysis is undertaken to simulate real world situations where several variables change simultaneously.
4. The project investor seeks to protect against the unfavorable states of the world by implementing appropriate risk mitigation measures.

GLOSSARY OF NEW TERMS

Certainty equivalent A certain risk-free amount of cash acceptable to investors in place of a (larger) amount conditioned with a degree of risk, slated to be received at the same point in time.

Risk Premium Incremental return offered to persuade investors to absorb additional risk.

Scenario Analysis A procedure to evaluate a change in the outcome, given a change in multiple input variables

Sensitivity Analysis A procedure to evaluate a change in the outcome, given a change in an input variable, holding other things constant.

Simulation A planning technique involving drawing up future states of the world to assess project risk.

Born Again: The Antonov Mriya

The Antonov An-225 Mriya ("Inspiration" or "Dream" in Ukrainian) is the largest operational aircraft ever built, even larger than the Airbus A380, as measured by gross take-off weight of 640 tonnes, and features on the Guinness Book of World Records for its 240 records. The An-225 is commercially available for flying any over-sized payload due to the singular design of its cargo deck and its powerplant capacity. In January 2002, the colossal aircraft flew to Oman with 216,000 prepared meals, weighing a shade under 200 tons, for American military personnel operating in the region. Beginning in June 2003, the An-225 and the rest of the Antonov fleet, helped deliver over 800 tons of equipment and humanitarian aid to war-torn Iraq. The US and Canadian governments have regularly availed of the services of the An-225 to supply coalition forces in the Middle East*.

The Mriya is a highly reliable transporter with the Antonov Airlines fleet, moving large objects such as locomotives and 150 ton generators, hitherto considered impossible to airlift. It has also made outstanding contributions to disaster relief operations by delivering huge quantities of emergency supplies in quick time. Yet, it is difficult

---

*   *http://en.wikipedia.org/wiki/Antonov_An-225*

(Continued)

to envision that the designers had such noble intentions in mind when the behemoth was conceptualized. Least of all, serving American troops in war zones, for, the Mriya was designed at the height of the cold war in the 1980s to carry the Energia rocket's boosters and the Soviet Buran space shuttle orbiter. The transporter was grounded following the collapse of the Soviet Union and the suspension of the Buran space program. Had it been a private initiative, the abrupt grounding of the Mriya would have wiped out billions of dollars in shareholder wealth.

In May 2001, the An-225 flew again, over a decade after being grounded[†] and the cargo service is now operated jointly by Ukrainian Antanov Airlines and the British firm Air Foyle. Since then, the demand for transporting super-heavy cargo has exceeded available capacity, and a second An-225 is being made airworthy. In addition to transporting aircraft parts, trucks and power station equipment, the company hopes to offer the Mriya as a launch platform to cash-in on the emerging space tourism industry.

Such opportunities might appear serendipitous, as the aircraft which was originally a technology showcase was left out in the cold, quite literally, with the collapse of the former Soviet Union. Projects are exposed to uncertain future states of the world, which cannot be predicted accurately on the day of making the investment. The collapse of the USSR and the emergence of new market segments for the An-225 could be extreme events. Yet, each project is exposed to changing fortunes, ranging from drifts in traffic volumes to swings in commodity prices. Analysts attempt to simulate future states of the world by altering project variables and arriving at the least preferred situations. In essence, a potential investor is keen to model the worst-case scenario and to put appropriate mitigation measures in place to ward off such a melt-down. This chapter and the next consider the various risks a project is exposed to, and outline measures to combat such uncertainty.

---

†   *http://news.bbc.co.uk/1/hi/world/europe/1317779.stm*

Introduction

The assessment of a project involves making educated guesses of future states of the world. Variables impacting the project are simulated and their evolution estimated, basing on past trends and present-day expectations for the future. Yet, the future seldom turns out precisely as anticipated.

This chapter highlights the uncertainties associated with predictions for the future. Since the investment decision is ultimately based on expected outcomes derived from future values of select variables, a significant step in the appraisal process is to identify the key variables likely to have a major impact on the project. The situation is further complicated by the longer time horizons involved in major infrastructure projects such as bridges and dams. The volatility implicit in designing long-term forecasts could be unnerving. Drawing on inferences relating to such variables to simulate outcomes, the best, worst, and most likely scenarios are then generated. The potential investor seeks to identify the worst case scenarios and to put adequate and appropriate safeguards in place to protect against less-preferred situations.

Dailami and Leipziger (1998) have studied infrastructure project finance and have examined the determination of credit risk premium, especially in developing countries. They observe that the market imposes a high risk premium on loans to countries with high inflation—which could be a signal of weak macroeconomic management, and specifically to projects in the road sector—probably owing to the high level of asset specificity. It is also observed that while evaluating long-term projects, investors make use of objective as well as subjective factors and more significantly, also differ in the selection of data used to support the ultimate decision. People differ in their perception and evaluation of the appraisal process itself and perceptions of risk are also deeply influenced by their cultural backgrounds, (De Camprieu, 2007).

Sensitivity Analysis

Sensitivity analysis computes the change in the decision signal viz., the NPV, IRR etc., given a change in one of the cash-flow elements viz., the retail price of the service to be delivered. As the very name goes, it enables a project analyst study the sensitivity of the project's return to a single variable. A key element in conducting the sensitivity analysis is taking a view on the "best estimate" or an "estimated range of values" for the variable in question – holding all other inputs constant. The range of estimated values normally spans either side of the base case projection. It is believed that experience in the industry sector and detailed market research would help devise estimates. The analyst then raises "what if" questions in which the financial model's output is reworked for each of the values of the selected input variable. In order to provide a pictorial guide, it is also useful to generate curves with the input (dependent) variable and the outcome (viz., IRR) to demonstrate the relationship between the two. A steep slope of the input-outcome curve indicates that the outcome is very sensitive to changes in the particular input, and vice versa, as illustrated in figure 6.1.

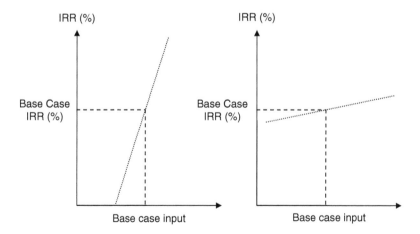

Figure 6.1: Sensitivity of IRR to two input variables: IRR is more sensitive to the first

The sensitivity analysis provides an investor with an indicative margin of error, in the estimates of project parameters, outside of which the projected outcome is reversed and the investment decision would need to be revisited. The evolution of spreadsheet software has made it very convenient for decision makers to undertake sensitivity analyses and to focus on key variables that could prove critical to the project's success. In addition to varying the magnitude of the input variables, (Table 6.1) it is also possible to alter the timing of events, viz., delay in construction and consequent delay in realising cash-flows etc.

The sensitivity of the wind turbine acquisition to the cost of long-term debt is analyzed, holding other variables constant. The range of possible input values is drawn from experience and expectations for the future. We observe from the graphical depiction in Figure 6.2 that the equity IRR curve is steeper than the project IRR implying that the equity holders' returns are more sensitive to the cost of long-term debt.

The sensitivity analysis suffers a few shortcomings as well. The foremost being the definition of the range of input values for a given variable. For instance, if a given long-term project were sensitive to market prices of a commodity as volatile as crude oil, an analyst would be unable to arrive at a convincing range of future prices. "In defining the uncertainty encompassing a given project variable, one should widen the uncertainty margins to account for the lack of sufficient data or the inherent errors contained in the base data used in making the prediction", (Savvides, 1994).

Table 6.1: Sensitivity of equity and project returns to cost of long-term debt (base case highlighted)

Cost of Debt	Equity IRR	Project IRR
9.00%	10.570%	10.443%
10.00%	10.325%	10.268%
11.00%	10.084%	10.095%
12.00%	9.846%	9.923%
13.00%	9.613%	9.753%
14.00%	9.384%	9.585%

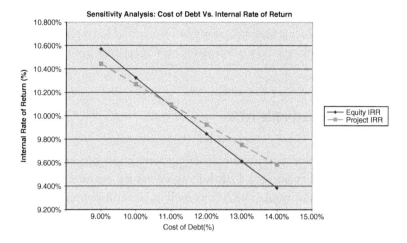

Figure 6.2: Sensitivity of equity and project IRR

In general, one-of-a-kind and first-of-its-kind projects do not benefit from past experience with the possible range of input values. Further, while input variables are varied in turn, all other parameters are held constant. The sensitivity of a project to a certain variable is a true reflection *if and only if* the other variables remain constant as projected.

Scenario Analysis

To address some of the shortcomings identified with the sensitivity analysis, scenarios are developed by altering multiple variables simultaneously. It is thus possible for an analyst to draw-up the best and worst cases for the project – future states of the world where all the input variables move favorably or unfavorably. With the base case being the "most likely" scenario and with the worst and best cases designed, the expected value is computed as an arithmetic average, weighted by the probabilities assigned to each scenario. Note that the "expected value" is a risk weighted statistical measure and not actually an anticipated outcome in itself.

The financial model developed over the previous chapters can be employed to conduct a scenario analysis. We are able to change several variables all at once to study the impact on the returns generated by the project.

Certainty Equivalents

A project investment produces cash-flows which can be predicted with a limited degree of accuracy. Computing certainty-equivalent amounts helps the analyst eliminate the risk as well as the compensation for such risk and arrive at a more deterministic stream of future cash-flows from the project.

If the cash-flow projected at the end of year 1 is INR 1000 with a certain degree of risk associated, and if a potential investor would be willing to accept INR 900 with complete certainty, then the INR 900 would be termed the 'certainty equivalent'. A potential investor is indifferent between a higher risky payout and a lower but certain payout. The certainty-equivalent factor for the given illustration would be INR 900 / INR 1000 or 0.9. It could serve as a measure of the embedded risk premium being demanded, wherein each INR 1000 of uncertain cash-flow is valued as being equivalent to INR 900 of certain cash-flow. Further, the present values of a stream of risk-free cash-flows discounted at the risk-free rate and a stream of risky cash-flows discounted at the cost of capital should be identical.

$$\frac{INR\ 900}{(1+R_f)^1} = \frac{INR\ 1000}{(1+WACC)^1}$$

$$\Rightarrow a_1 . \frac{INR\ 1000}{(1+R_f)^1} = \frac{INR\ 1000}{(1+WACC)^1}$$

$$\Rightarrow a_1 = \frac{(1+R_f)^1}{(1+WACC)^1} \quad \text{or} \quad a_t = \frac{(1+R_f)^t}{(1+WACC)^t}$$

Where a_t is the certainty-equivalent factor, whose magnitude diminishes over time, implying that the project's cash-flows from afar are more risky and less valuable than immediate payouts. Mehra (2006) has computed, (Table 6.2) the risk premium for Indian conditions and has reported the equity premium (risk compensation) relative to the bank deposit rate which is used as a proxy for a risk-free security.

Table 6.2: Risk Premium for Indian Markets: Extract from Mehra (2006)

	India Returns: 1991 - 2004				
	Relatively Risk-Less Security	BSE 100	Equity Premium (BSE 100)	BSE Sensex	Equity Premium (Sensex)
Mean Real Return (%)	1.28	12.6	11.3	11.0	9.7
Standard Deviation (%)	1.73	37.2	37.7	32.6	33.2

Probability Distributions

Project risk is defined as the degree of divergence or variability between the expected outcome and the actual outcome. The larger the uncertainty associated with the quantum and timing of project cash-flows, larger is the potential variability, and greater the risk to be borne by investors. Potential investors 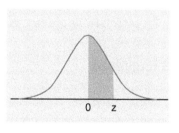 are therefore primarily concerned with the variability of outcomes, predominantly, the risk of the project underperforming. Assuming that the range of eventual outcomes is 'normally' distributed, the normal curve can be used to ascertain the probability of the project generating less than expected returns.

A range of possible values (from minimum to maximum) for each risk variable is defined, which sets boundaries for the probability distribution. Taking cues from historical observations and projecting them into the foreseeable future helps develop the frequency distribution required. Yet it is usually imperative to rely on experience, intuition and judgment to project values of subjective factors and is normally determined in discussion with observers and subject experts. A suitable probability distribution profile is selected – in most cases the 'normal' distribution is considered owing to familiarity, convenience and relative accuracy – to describe the variability profile of the project input variable.

Correlated Variables

The analyst needs to pay special attention to the presence of correlated input variables. In the DND Flyway case discussed at the beginning of chapter 3, the toll and the traffic volumes are correlated (negatively) implying that when the toll rises, the traffic volumes fall and vice versa. If the probability assigned is not adjusted to reflect the correlation, it is entirely possible that unrealistic scenarios are generated wherein, the price and the quantity rise simultaneously. Setting correlation conditions for such variables ensures that scenarios violative of such correlations are not generated.

Simulations

The risk variables are selected randomly within the specified ranges and in conformance with given probability distributions to compute the project outcome – the IRR or the NPV. These values are stored after each run of 'random' input generation. The accumulated results from the numerous runs – usually of the order of several thousand – are stored for statistical analysis.

The wind turbine acquisition project under evaluation is thought to involve a medium degree of risk. The upfront investment (year 0) is

INR 1000 lakh (INR 100 million). The normal distribution can be illustrated by simulating anticipated conditions and the corresponding probabilities.

We then compute the Variance as $(NPV-\text{Expected }NPV)^2 * \text{Probability}$ and the Standard Deviation as the square root of the Variance. Probability of a negative NPV can be computed from: $(0-\text{Expected }NPV)/ \text{Std Deviation}$. Probability of negative project NPV:

$$\frac{(0.0-161.0872)}{145.1920} = 1.10948 \text{ std. units}$$

Probability of a negative project NPV is given by the area under the normal curve, Table 6A at the end of this chapter. Given the possible range of values assumed and the probability distribution assigned to the cost of project debt, there is a 86.65% probability that the project will generate a return less than the cost of capital.

Cost of Debt	Probability	Project NPV
0.00%	0.15	91.1925
6.00%	0.20	-54.3378
11.00%	0.30	-176.3797
16.00%	0.20	-279.3256
21.00%	0.15	-367.4632
Expected NPV		-161.0872
Variance		21080.7279
Std Deviation		145.1920

Probability distributions used in risk analysis help communicate the odds for various outcomes better. Major issues potentially impacting project outcomes are identified and resolved by assigning numerical values. The investor is better equipped to commit funds, given the probability of such outcomes. On identifying the various sources of risk and the probability of their emergence computed, the proponent is able to design contractual structures to pass on such risks to agencies best suited to managing them.

Conclusion

A critical aspect of project appraisal and investment decision making is identifying significant risks and the probabilities associated with the occurrence of such adverse events. The sponsor is then in a position to enlist the mitigation measures best suited to the context. Risk management involves allocating risks through contractual structures to the agencies best suited to managing them. Where a counter party is involved, for instance, the contracts could provide for penalties for delays and defaults. Alternatively, where natural elements such as rains are vital for the success of the project, as with hydro-electric power plants, appropriate weather related insurance contracts could be procured. Innovations in the globalized world of finance such as currency futures, swaps and derivative instruments help project sponsors manage risk better. The next chapter deals with risk management measures.

References

Dailami, Mansoor and Leipziger, Danny "Infrastructure Project Finance and Capital Flows: A New Perspective", World Development, Vol. 26 (7), July 1998, p 1283 – 1298.

De Camprieu, Renaud. Desbiens, Jacques and Feixue, Yang "Cultural Differences in Project Risk Perception: An Empirical Comparison of China and Canada", International Journal of Project Management, Vol. 25 (7), October 2007, p 683 – 693.

Mehra, Rajnish "The Equity Premium in India", National Bureau of Economic Research, Working Paper No.12434, August 2006, http://www.nber.org/papers/w12434.

Savvides, Savvakis C. "Risk Analysis in Investment Appraisal", Project Appraisal, Vol 9, No.1, p 3 – 18, March 1994.

Table 6A: Area under the normal curve

Area between 0 and z

	0.00	0.01	0.02	0.03	0.04	0.05	0.06	0.07	0.08	0.09
0.0	0.0000	0.0040	0.0080	0.0120	0.0160	0.0199	0.0239	0.0279	0.0319	0.0359
0.1	0.0398	0.0438	0.0478	0.0517	0.0557	0.0596	0.0636	0.0675	0.0714	0.0753
0.2	0.0793	0.0832	0.0871	0.0910	0.0948	0.0987	0.1026	0.1064	0.1103	0.1141
0.3	0.1179	0.1217	0.1255	0.1293	0.1331	0.1368	0.1406	0.1443	0.1480	0.1517
0.4	0.1554	0.1591	0.1628	0.1664	0.1700	0.1736	0.1772	0.1808	0.1844	0.1879
0.5	0.1915	0.1950	0.1985	0.2019	0.2054	0.2088	0.2123	0.2157	0.2190	0.2224
0.6	0.2257	0.2291	0.2324	0.2357	0.2389	0.2422	0.2454	0.2486	0.2517	0.2549
0.7	0.2580	0.2611	0.2642	0.2673	0.2704	0.2734	0.2764	0.2794	0.2823	0.2852
0.8	0.2881	0.2910	0.2939	0.2967	0.2995	0.3023	0.3051	0.3078	0.3106	0.3133
0.9	0.3159	0.3186	0.3212	0.3238	0.3264	0.3289	0.3315	0.3340	0.3365	0.3389
1.0	0.3413	0.3438	0.3461	0.3485	0.3508	0.3531	0.3554	0.3577	0.3599	0.3621
1.1	0.3643	0.3665	0.3686	0.3708	0.3729	0.3749	0.3770	0.3790	0.3810	0.3830
1.2	0.3849	0.3869	0.3888	0.3907	0.3925	0.3944	0.3962	0.3980	0.3997	0.4015
1.3	0.4032	0.4049	0.4066	0.4082	0.4099	0.4115	0.4131	0.4147	0.4162	0.4177
1.4	0.4192	0.4207	0.4222	0.4236	0.4251	0.4265	0.4279	0.4292	0.4306	0.4319
1.5	0.4332	0.4345	0.4357	0.4370	0.4382	0.4394	0.4406	0.4418	0.4429	0.4441
1.6	0.4452	0.4463	0.4474	0.4484	0.4495	0.4505	0.4515	0.4525	0.4535	0.4545
1.7	0.4554	0.4564	0.4573	0.4582	0.4591	0.4599	0.4608	0.4616	0.4625	0.4633
1.8	0.4641	0.4649	0.4656	0.4664	0.4671	0.4678	0.4686	0.4693	0.4699	0.4706

(Continued)

Table 6A: Area under the normal curve (Continued)

	Area between 0 and z									
	0.00	0.01	0.02	0.03	0.04	0.05	0.06	0.07	0.08	0.09
1.9	0.4713	0.4719	0.4726	0.4732	0.4738	0.4744	0.4750	0.4756	0.4761	0.4767
2.0	0.4772	0.4778	0.4783	0.4788	0.4793	0.4798	0.4803	0.4808	0.4812	0.4817
2.1	0.4821	0.4826	0.4830	0.4834	0.4838	0.4842	0.4846	0.4850	0.4854	0.4857
2.3	0.4893	0.4896	0.4898	0.4901	0.4904	0.4906	0.4909	0.4911	0.4913	0.4916
2.4	0.4918	0.4920	0.4922	0.4925	0.4927	0.4929	0.4931	0.4932	0.4934	0.4936
2.5	0.4938	0.4940	0.4941	0.4943	0.4945	0.4946	0.4948	0.4949	0.4951	0.4952
2.6	0.4953	0.4955	0.4956	0.4957	0.4959	0.4960	0.4961	0.4962	0.4963	0.4964
2.7	0.4965	0.4966	0.4967	0.4968	0.4969	0.4970	0.4971	0.4972	0.4973	0.4974
2.8	0.4974	0.4975	0.4976	0.4977	0.4977	0.4978	0.4979	0.4979	0.4980	0.4981
2.9	0.4981	0.4982	0.4982	0.4983	0.4984	0.4984	0.4985	0.4985	0.4986	0.4986
3.0	0.4987	0.4987	0.4987	0.4988	0.4988	0.4989	0.4989	0.4989	0.4990	0.4990

Management of Project Risk

KEY CHAPTER CONCEPTS

1. Investors and lenders seek to protect against less preferred states of the world by undertaking appropriate risk management measures.

2. In situations where the risk cannot be allocated to a uniquely identified legal entity, as with weather related risks, insurance contracts serve to eliminate volatility in project cash flows.

3. Among the risks facing a project, the revenue risk is perhaps the most significant and has to be allocated most efficiently to provide requisite comfort to private sector investors.

4. Having multiple 'liquidity' options is vital for external equity investors, especially in developing countries, where project sponsors are less well-endowed, markets are shallow and cross-border movement of currencies tends to be restrained by law.

GLOSSARY OF NEW TERMS

Annuity The receipt (or payment) of a series of equal cash-amounts per accounting period, for a defined tenure.

Hedging Entering into a contract or setting up a structure to offset a recognized risk and to mitigate volatility in project cash-flows.

Liquidity Event An investor's route for "cashing out" of an investment, possibly through a strategic sale or a public offering of equity shares; also known as the 'harvest strategy' or the 'exit strategy'

Swap A contract obligating the parties involved to exchange specified cash-flows at specified points in time.

Take-or-Pay Contract A contract imposing an unconditional obligation on the client to pay for the good or service irrespective of whether the client actually consumes the same.

Risk–Return Tradeoff: The Golden Quadrilateral Road Network

The Panagarh-Palsit highway project in West Bengal, forming part of the India's ambitious Golden Quadrilateral national highway network was taken up as a model annuity based build-operate-transfer (BOT) project. Under the annuity system, the project developer is paid a fixed amount by the contracting authority, for a pre-determined period.

The National Highways Authority of India (NHAI) had carried out the feasibility assessment for the project prior to inviting global tenders from interested developers. The estimated cost of construction, operation and maintenance of the facilities and the expected financial returns form the basis for the competing annuity bids. The contract was awarded to the bidder with the lowest quote for the annuity[*]. Gamuda Bhd of Malaysia[†], has been responsible for the design, supervision, construction and upgrade of the two-lane road to a 64 km four-lane highway. The $460m project included the construction of service roads, several culverts, a rail over bridge, underpasses, bus shelters and other wayside amenities and toll plazas. The developer expects to recoup and earn a return on the initial investment through the semi-annual payments received from NHAI for a period of 15 years[‡]. However, despite the fact that the private-sector

---

[*]   *Based on Singh and Kalidindi (2006)*
[†]   *www.gamuda.com.my*
[‡]   *Manoj (2001)*

(*Continued*)

developer is not exposed to revenue uncertainty, the annuity quotes received were far higher than NHAI estimates. The episode illustrates the complexity involved in investing in road projects in developing countries, owing largely to the asset specificity and the length of the payback period.

Project risks are allocated to agents best equipped to absorb and manage such risks, through the influence or control on the inputs potentially leading to the uncertain outcomes. Alternatively, such risks are passed on to project participants who can easily insure or hedge the risks and thus spread the risk over the many. In most infrastructure projects, the host government absorbs the risks relating to the most sensitive parameters to help allay legitimate concerns of the private-sector participants.

The 64 km stretch is merely a pilot, to help expedite the rollout of the national highway network. It has soon become apparent that such road projects are exposed to different categories of risks at various stages of development. The traffic revenue risk is the most critical and yet stakeholders are often unable to decide on the agency best suited to absorb such risk. The traffic-revenue risk is borne by the private sector developer in the DND Flyway project discussed at the beginning of chapter 3. The annuity model, on the other hand, insulates the developer from the project's revenue risk. Analysts have opined that in the interest of making more efficient use of tax-payer money, the annuity payouts should be indexed to input prices, long-term interest costs etc, so as to achieve more realistic payment streams.

Introduction

Investments made towards the development, construction and operation of an infrastructure project are recovered from government grants and user fees. Most private sector developers would prefer to err on the side of caution and allocate the cash-flow risks involved, to other agencies.

This chapter provides an overview of the risk mitigation and management measures available to project developers. The annuity model discussed in the case above is one such method of allocating the revenue risk to the host government. Financial engineering is extensively employed to help manage the volatility in interest rates, currency exchange rates, commodity prices and other parameters likely to impact the viability of a project. Complex derivative products are fashioned using the basic building blocks: options, swaps, forwards and futures. Such instruments reduce volatility in earnings and help sponsors eliminate down-side risks. It is possible to design contractual structures to allocate risks to counter- parties, viz., delays and cost overruns in construction or to third parties viz., revenue risks to governments. In situations where the counter-party is not a uniquely identifiable legal entity, as with weather related events and *force majeure*, project risks could be curtailed by executing insurance contracts with reputed insurers.

Construction Risks

The construction contracts for flow-type projects — railroads, road networks, pipelines etc., are allocated to construction companies and engineering-procurement-construction (EPC) contractors, involving performance testing, obtaining necessary permits, managing on-site issues and procuring contractors' all risk insurance policies. Under an EPC contract, the contractor accepts full responsibility for delivering an operational facility at defined quality, on time and at contracted cost. The contractor is normally required to compensate the project in events of delays, for the consequent interest costs and for the loss in income to project sponsors. Contractor liability is generally capped at a certain proportion of the construction contract price, often in the range of 10% - 15%, (Ruster, 1996). Material, workmanship and equipment quality and operation are generally warrantied for a defect-liability period of 1–2 years. A pre-determined proportion of the payable invoice amounts, say 5%, is retained in an escrow account to provide comfort to the lenders and sponsors.

Operating Risks

Projects such as power plants are exposed to the possibility that the clients, normally state-owned utilities and transmission companies, fail to draw on the power produced. Such risks are more acute in market situations involving sole buyers ("monopsony"). *Take-or-pay* contracts require the client to pay for the good or service, irrespective of whether it is actually drawn and / or consumed. In other situations, the contract is backed up by a more credible guarantee, viz., a federal guarantee to provide the requisite comfort for the investor. Conversely, raw material supplies are secured through *put-or-pay* contracts. Suppliers indemnify the project company against loss of revenue or additional costs incurred on account of supply disruptions. A *pass-through* arrangement helps the project company pass on higher prices of feedstock to the client. The price escalation formula is normally indexed against internationally acknowledged reference prices.

Financial Risks

Managing the risks associated with the financial parameters associated with the project, viz., interest rates, currency exchange rates, equity valuations and exit strategies etc., call for ingenuity and astute financial engineering skills. Several instruments have been developed, which could be employed in isolation or in combination to minimize the down-side risks for the project and to eliminate volatility in cash-flow patterns. These include swaps, options, futures and forwards.

Swaps

A swap contract obligates the parties involved to exchange specified cash-flows at specified points in time. In an interest-rate swap, the cash flows are computed basing on two different interest rates – usually one fixed and one floating - charged on the same currency. A currency swap involves the exchange of cash flow streams in two different currencies.

Interest Rate Swaps

The parties to an interest-rate swap agree to exchange interest payment obligations: usually swapping floating and fixed liabilities. One of the parties might be liable to pay a specified rate, say 6.0%, while the other a floating rate, linked to a benchmark interest rate such as the London Inter-Bank Offer Rate (LIBOR). The coupon payments are swapped, with a view to aligning the liabilities with the respective party's receivables. The two parties do not exchange the principal and the compliance is simultaneous. If one party defaults on its contracted obligation, the other is automatically released from its commitment.

Assuming that the toll road project discussed at the beginning of the chapter is exposed to annuity revenue streams that are indexed to the cost of borrowing, the project would be better off paying floating interest rates, so as to match its cash inflow patterns. However, if a lender were keen on a fixed rate loan, the project could choose to swap the interest payments with yet another project ("project B") which has floating rate obligations. Assuming that the notional principal is INR 100 crore, the interest payment at a fixed rate of 6.0% is INR 6.0 crore. Assuming that project B, with a floating rate obligation, is required to pay 5.5%, its interest charge on the notional principal is INR 5.5 crore. To net off liabilities, project B pays the road project INR 0.5 crore. Project B's total payout, therefore is INR 6.0 crore, comprising the INR 5.5 crore it pays its lender and the INR 0.5 crore it pays the road project.

In six months, assuming that the benchmark has moved to 7.0%, the road project would be required to pay INR 1.0 crore to project B. Project B, therefore pays the lender INR 6.0 crore and passes through the INR 1.0 crore received from the road project. In both situations, project B has a fixed outflow of INR 6.0 crore. Conversely, the road project receives or pays out interest differentials between the fixed and floating rates.

Interest-rate swaps are employed to eliminate uncertainty (floating to fixed) associated with floating rates and to align outflows with revenue patterns (fixed / floating). A swap of this nature is effectively used when the project's lender (or consortium of banks) prefers to offer floating rate loans, while the project itself earns fixed annuities. The lenders' own preferences are linked to the risk profiles of the projects and the credit rating of the sponsors in question. With increasing sophistication, swaps are generally packaged with other products (currency swaps, interest rate swaps, options etc.) and managed by large banks and financial institutions.

Currency Swaps

The parties to a currency swap—generally with revenue streams denominated in their respective home currencies - agree to exchange a series of specified payment obligations denominated in the other's home currency with payments in respective home currencies. Commonly, the currency swap could be effected with large modern day commercial banks having exposures in several currencies. While overcoming the associated exchange rate uncertainty, such swaps could be necessary to overcome regulatory rigidities preventing flows of currencies across national borders, or to benefit from prevailing tax structures.

If Tata Steel, an Indian company, seeks to make an investment in the United Kingdom, and say, British Telecom (BT) intends to invest in the Indian market, the firms could borrow in their respective home currencies, the Indian Rupee and the British Pound, respectively and enter into a currency swap.

Assuming that a 10-year British Pound debt to BT costs 10%, while a ten-year Indian Rupee loan is available to Tata Steel at 8%, and the companies agree to swap their principal and interest obligations:

1. Tata Steel borrows INR 1 billion and exchanges it with BT for GB £125 million (at the prevailing exchanging rate of INR 80 / GB £).

2. In each year following the initial exchange, Tata Steel undertakes to pay BT the debt service of £12.5m (10% * £125m). Conversely, BT undertakes to pay Tata Steel INR 80m (8% * INR 1b), to service the debt in India.

3. In year ten, at the end of the contract period, the initial transaction is reversed. Tata Steel pays BT £ 12.5m, while BT pays Tata Steel INR 1billion.

4. In reality, one party pays the other the difference between the amounts due ("netting out") basing on the prevailing exchange rates.

Effectively, Tata Steel borrows and repays in Indian Rupees but gets to utilize and service a GB £ loan. The reverse holds true for British Telecom.

Options

The holder of an option has the right but not the obligation to undertake a particular transaction. A *call* option is the right to buy ("call" for) an asset. A *put* option bestows the right to sell an asset. The strike or exercise price is the price at which the option holder may choose to buy or sell the underlying asset, on or before the expiration date of the option. The option holder walks away from the transaction when the option is out-of-the-money i.e, when exercising the option does not lead to a gain.

Call Options

A steel company could acquire a call option from the government on an ore mining site. At the end of the contract period, the company could choose to exercise the option depending on whether the contracted price is lower than the prevailing market price. Exercising the in-the-money option helps the company make a profit equal to the difference between the prevailing market price and the exercise price. If the prevailing market price is lower, the company simply acquires the site at the market price and the option expires unexercised.

Put Options

A put option works like an insurance policy and gives the option-holder the right to *sell* an asset at a pre-determined price within a prescribed time horizon. The asset owner acquires a put option so as to secure a minimum price realization on the sale of the asset. The purchaser of the option chooses to exercise it when the prevailing market price for the asset is lower than the exercise price i.e. the option is "in-the-money". If the prevailing price is higher, the put option goes unutilized.

Forwards and Futures

A Forward contract obligates the parties involved, to exchange a specified amount of a particular asset — usually agricultural produce, commodities or currencies — at a stated price, determined at the time of entering into the contract. The parties to the contract gain or lose depending on the evolution of the market price for the commodity or currency in question. If the market price is higher than the contracted purchase price, the contract holder gains the difference. Conversely, the seller loses an equal amount. Forward contracts generally involve buyers who are interested in taking physical delivery of the traded commodity. Consequently, forward contracts are usually exposed to default risk by either party – the seller could fail to come up with the goods, while the buyer could default on the purchase commitment. Insurance contracts, especially for agricultural commodities, and escrow mechanisms could alleviate such concerns.

Forward Rate Agreements

A forward rate agreement (FRA) on a project loan functions in a similar fashion. A project company could lock-in a specified interest rate for a loan it hopes to draw at some point in the future. This is generally effective when perceptions relating to the future movements in interest rates differ. If the lenders believe that interest rates are likely to be depressed while the borrowers perceive that rates are likely to rise, a forward rate agreement is mutually beneficial. However, depending on the actual evolution of the interest rates, one party gains and the other loses in equal measure.

The borrower could also procure an option contract with the lender to call the loan in due course, at a pre-defined interest rate. If the market rates are lower, the option could retire unutilized. If the market rates are higher than the exercise rates on or before the option's expiration date, the option is 'in the money' and the borrower chooses to cash-in.

Futures

Unlike a Forwards contract where cash-flows materialise on the contract termination date, a Futures contract involves 'marking-to-market', a day to day adjustment of gains and losses. The futures contracts are standardised and traded on organized exchanges and cover precious metals, industrial and agricultural commodities, currencies, stock-market indices, etc. Most futures contracts are cash settled. Alternatively, contracts are closed prematurely if the party concerned does not maintain margins mandated by the exchanges. Future markets are more liquid compared to forwards because they are standardised exchange traded products, and do not generally require physical delivery of the underlying asset.

Securing an Exit for the Equity Investors

A project company, by definition, does not require intermediate investments and generally has free-cash to distribute from early on. In order of priority, project debt is repaid first and the security offered to the lender is released. Similarly, the preference shares could be redeemed progressively or converted into common equity in accordance with an agreed formula.

The challenge lies in offering individual and institutional equity investors an exit from a project. The first alternative normally considered is a *put* option agreement with the project's sponsors, who would prefer to stay invested. The put option agreement provides for the acquisition of the outgoing investors' shares in accordance with a pre-agreed formula, within a prescribed time window. In order to secure the sponsors' commitment, an escrow account is built up to make requisite funds available to effect the buyback.

If buyback is beyond the reasonable capacity of the sponsors and / or if the sponsors themselves seek to partly exit the project, a liquidity event is contemplated. This could be in the form of an initial public offering (IPO) for the project company, followed by a listing on reputed stock exchanges. Sponsors and external investors could offload a part of their equity stakes subsequently.

Alternatively, when project operations have stabilized and cash-flow patterns are more stable and predictable, the project could issue bonds to substitute some of the equity with long-term debt. Retiring a part of the equity with the issue of project-specific bonds could also be combined with a put option to enable the external investor to exit the project.

In certain situations, the transaction costs involved in a public offering of bonds or equity shares could be prohibitive and out of proportion with the project itself. Under such circumstances, the external investors should look at other liquidity options. One such could be a strategic sale of the stake to third party investors intending to enter the project. A strategic sale is generally subject to the sponsors' right of first refusal, and is brought about when the third-party's entry is likely to add significant value to project operations.

External investors such as private equity players and venture capital funds tend to invest in several projects within the same geography, to hedge their bets. All such stakes are owned by a "holding company", which in effect is a portfolio management company, with no real world operations of its own. An additional liquidity opportunity available to equity investors and venture capital funds would be to make a public offering of shares in the holding company to realize value from the investment.

Conclusion

Hedging project risks with the help of options, futures, forwards or swaps reduces the down-side risks to a project and cuts out the volatility in projected cash-flows. The instruments are generally used in combination with insurance contracts to ward off unforeseen environmental, social and *force majeure* risks.

Project sponsors prefer to mitigate uncertainty, even it if is associated with an upfront cost, compared to suffering the consequences of unforeseen adverse outcomes. Derivative securities are useful in hedging commodity price risks in stock-type projects where metal and mineral prices could prove to be volatile. Futures contracts on currencies could help when incomes and liabilities are denominated in different currencies.

Redemption of preference shares and repayment of project debt is relatively straightforward. Exit from projects is a significant risk for external equity investors and planning liquidity events well in advance could help mitigate the same. In addition to selling the stake to the project's promoters, external investors could also choose to make a strategic sale of their stake to third parties or to liquidate a part of their shareholding in the investment holding company.

References

Manoj, P. 'Panagarh-Palsit Project – Potholes on Annuity Approach Road', The Hindu BusinessLine 30 January 2001.

Ruster, Jeff 'Mitigating Commercial Risks in Project Finance', Private Sector Development Department, The World Bank, Note No. 69, February 1996.

Singh, Boeing L. and Kalidindi S. N. 'Traffic Revenue Risk Management Through Annuity Model of PPP Road Projects in India', *International Journal of Project Management*, Vol. 24, 2006, p 605 – 613.

Risk and Real Options in Project Appraisal

KEY CHAPTER CONCEPTS

1. Traditional project evaluation techniques involve a single decision point, while the *real-options analysis* considers multiple decision-points.

2. At each stage, sponsors collect additional information which helps them make the "proceed" vs. "abandon" decision.

3. The decision tree is used to determine the probability weighted present value of future outcomes.

4. The option space is a two-dimensional diagrammatic representation of the value-to-cost metric and the associated volatility, used to grade projects in the order of their increasing attractiveness.

5. Assigning an economic value to options embedded in project proposals could reverse investment decisions that are originally based on traditional discounted-cash-flow analyses.

GLOSSARY OF NEW TERMS

Decision Tree: A strategic planning tool depicting the evolution of possible project outcomes over time.

Embedded Option: A project implicitly offers multiple decision points spread out in time, including the option to delay or abandon projects.

Option: A contract giving its holder the right to buy or sell an asset at a predetermined price during a defined time period.

Option Space: A pictorial representation of the project's value potential and the volatility associated.

Real Options: Real (tangible) investment choices available to investors.

Wait and Watch Options: Investment opportunities that could be availed of when additional information is gathered.

Options for Trans-Island Transportation

At US$ 18 billion in construction costs, the Taiwan North-South High Speed Rail Project (HSR) is perhaps the largest privately managed and funded build-operate-transfer (BOT) project implemented todate[*]. It is also the first time that the Japanese *Shinkansen* ("bullet train") was exported for an overseas project. The HSR links Taipei to Kaohsiung, a total length of 345km, to be covered in 90 minutes, running along the west coast of Taiwan. The line has 48 tunnels, (including one that is 7.5 km long), and in all, 62 km of track is underground while 73% of the line is elevated, (held aloft by 30,000 massive concrete supports), making the line the longest continuously elevated railway in the world. Since just 9% of the track was built on the ground, the project costs appear underestimated.

The HSR helps relieve traffic congestion while offering greater safety, high transit volumes, low land occupancy, energy efficiency and low pollution[†]. Beginning operations in January 2007, the service had clocked five million cumulative passengers by early June and over fifteen million before the end of the year.

---

[*]   *http://www.thsrc.com.tw/en/index.htm*
[†]   *http://en.wikipedia.org/wiki/Taiwan_High_Speed_Rail*

(Continued)

The concession is awarded to finance, construct and operate the HSR for a period of 35 years and the station area real estate development for 50 years. The project is funded with 20% equity and 80% project debt from local banking groups. The rail currently has a 50% load factor on weekdays and 60% on weekends, while the company expects to break-even at a 60% load while operating 88 trains per day. 98% of revenue accrues from fares while only 2% is non fare revenue from franchise stores in the stations, and from advertising in the stations and on the trains. A government imposed ceiling on ticket prices and the relatively small population of Taiwan are serious constraints on revenue growth[‡].

While construction costs were underestimated and passenger revenues overstated at the planning stage, achieving breakeven appears challenging, because expanding capacity would not necessarily attract additional passengers. The Taiwan HSR offers an interesting application of real options in evaluating large, long-term projects. A comprehensive analysis using actual project data confirms that the *real* value of the project is underestimated by the traditional cash-flow valuation[§]. The value placed by the Taiwan High-Speed Rail Consortium (THSRC), the operating company, on the flexibility to adapt decisions in the light of future contingencies is significant and necessary to justify the project's implementation. In addition to individual options, the interaction among such options adds value overlooked by static cash-flow methods.

Projects such as constructing a railway network, involving distinct stages of information-gathering and decision-making, are associated with options at each stage to continue or abandon the project. Traditional Net Present Value NPV analyses cannot capture the value of these real (tangible) options, because such methods involve only a single decision point. Multiple decision points take new information into account at each stage and update the value of the project basing on the new information. This approach is especially valuable in projects such as the HSR, as the expansion of the network could enhance traffic volumes and revenues on existing lines as well.

[‡]   *Knowledge at Wharton (2007)*
[§]   *Bowe and Lee (2004)*

Introduction

Projects are seldom implemented in one stretch. Stock-type projects involve depletion of the available reserve over time, while networks of flow-type projects are progressively expanded to cover larger areas.

The real-options technique deals with the analysis of a project with multiple decision-points and with assigning an economic value to these tangible decision-making opportunities. Exclusive reliance on the NPV or Internal rate of interest (IRR) decision signals ignores the value of such managerial flexibility and the opportunities to derive value from changing the course of the project over time. The existence of such opportunities enhances the value of the project to the equity investor.

Project Valuation with Embedded Options

The analysis of the real options embedded in a given project commences with the discounted cash-flows generated in the traditional way. Economic values are then ascribed to the options to arrive at the project's worth to a potential investor. The larger the number of decision points spread out in time, the greater the number of options and their contribution to the project's worth.

Total Project Value= NPV (from DCF analysis) + Value of real options

In practice, real options are treated as qualitative variables and their economic value is seldom reported in numerical terms alongside the decision signals. This is partly owing to the difficulty in fitting a valuation formula to such options. Ad hoc approaches such as decision trees and simulations are frequently used. On occasion, the scenario analyses *subsume* the real option methods without making explicit mention of the same.

The types of options include:

1. Stock-type projects: the option to vary production volumes over time, in keeping with market conditions. Production could be

expanded under favorable conditions and vice versa. The exercise of this option is readily observable in the international crude oil markets, where producers respond to price cues.

2. Assets with finite lives and the option to abandon: some project assets are worth more dead than alive and hence abandoning the project could be more valuable (or less costly) than keeping it operational. Ships are broken and aircraft components recycled when they are perceived to have outlived their utility, are found to be fuel-inefficient and/or pose serious safety concerns to passengers or cargo.

3. The wait and watch option: the option to postpone launch or expansion of a project gives investors additional time to assess evolving market conditions and to obtain additional information. This is valuable in both flow-type and stock-type projects.

Decision Trees

"When used as a strategic planning tool, decision analysis can help managers address issues such as how to allocate resources to ensure that the project meets specific deadlines, when to scale up or delay investments and when to exit a project", (D'Souza, 2002).

Strategic business decisions have a time profile to them i.e., they cannot generally be now-or-never decisions. Spreading the decision out in time provides decision makers the information to manage risk more effectively and the elimination of such uncertainty without depletion in the project's worth is valuable.

We illustrate the use of decision trees through a product development decision process. Imagine that an auto major decides to launch a new car model. The company estimates that it could modify existing facilities to produce 50,000 units over the first two years. However, this level of production is not scale-efficient. As a result, the project's NPV from classical discounted cash-flow analysis is -US$ 10 million.

However, if the car model turns out to be a winner, the company could invest in a dedicated facility two years hence, growing output to 100,000 units per annum, which would be a viable proposition. The company also perceives that without the initial investment, the first-mover advantage would be lost and the follow-on investment opportunity is not created.

Basing on managers' experience and judgment, the decision tree to capture the situation is drawn up. There is a 50–50 chance that the market would respond positively to the new offering. If it does, the NPV of the follow-on investment at the end of year 2 would be US$ 150m or about US$ 120m at present. If the market does not take-off, the follow-on investment is not made and the incremental NPV is zero.

The mean of the distribution of possible NPVs associated with the option discussed is $0.5*(\$120m) + 0.5(0) = US\$ 60m$

The project's total present worth, therefore stands at $\$-10m + \$60m = US \$50m$.

Clearly, even though the initial investment yields a negative NPV, the option to expand production compensates more than adequately. Decision trees facilitate the analysis of sequential decisions subject to chance events at future dates.

When multiple future decision points are involved, the optimal sequence of decisions is obtained by rolling back the tree from the right hand side. The most distant decisions are quantified first, followed sequentially by intermediate decisions, reaching the initial decision point.

Concerns with Decision Trees

The greatest concern with the use of decision trees in evaluating project opportunities is the assignment of probabilities to future events. Perceptions of chances of success or failure at individual stages of the

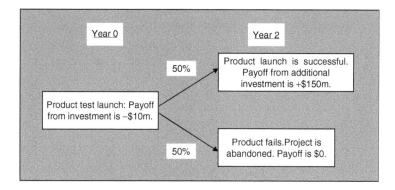

Figure 8.1: Decision Tree Illustrated

project could vary significantly among decision makers. Project proponents are likely to be more optimistic about the eventual outcome,
compared to potential lenders and investors. It is difficult to eliminate
such bias and arrive at an objective assessment, especially for large
stand-alone projects.

Option Space and Value Metrics

Yet another pictorial representation of the value associated with being
able to defer an investment is the *option space,* defined by two option-
value metrics[†]. The first metric is the value-to-cost or in other words,
the ratio of the project's NPV to the initial investment (profitability
index). When this measure is greater than 1, the project is worth more
than the investment it involves. The second metric is the volatility
measure which depends on the degree of uncertainty of the future value
of the assets in question. This metric quantifies the extent to which
things can change before an investment decision must be made and is
measured by variance per period of asset returns and the option's time
to expiration. The two measures are used to define the option space as
shown in Figure 8.2.

---

† *This section is based on Luehrman (1998)*

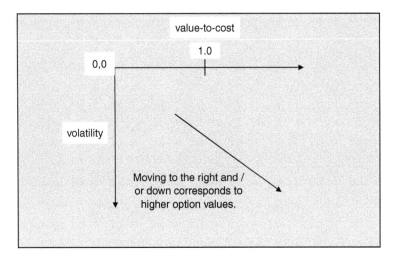

Figure 8.2: Option Space Layout

This option space is further subdivided into six separate regions, each with a distinct type of option and a corresponding decision recommendation, as shown in Figure 8.3.

- In regions 1 and 6, at the very top of the option space, the volatility metric is zero. The decision maker is *certain* about project outcomes

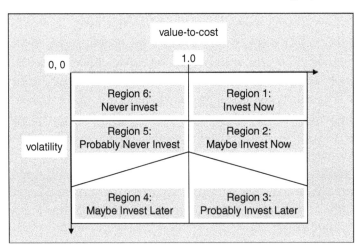

Figure 8.3: Locating projects in the Option Space

and hence the decision is either to invest (value-to-cost >1) or not to invest.

- In regions 2 and 3, projects are promising because the underlying assets are worth more than the required investment. The curve that separates the two regions is formed by points with NPV = 0. Projects in region 2 are 'in the money' while those in region 3 are presently 'out of the money'. Between regions 2 and 3, the investment decision requires a case-by-case comparison of the value of investing immediately versus delaying the proposed investment.

- All projects with a value-to-cost metric lower than 1 are deemed less promising. However, the option space helps us segregate the more preferred ones from the less valuable ones. While the high volatility associated with projects in region 3 could make it unattractive, the opposite could hold for projects in region 4. Project opportunities in region 5 suffer from low returns and a low possibility of turning more profitable at future dates.

The flexibility arising from the time available to exercise an option and the underlying uncertainty of future states of the world produce different assessments as compared to conventional methods of analyses. In all, placing a value on the option leads the analyst to delay the decision making on some of the projects, thus reserving the possibility of value generation commencing at a future date. When the available capital is to be rationed across projects, the options framework helps rank wait-and-see projects in order of their attractiveness. It is also possible to envisage situations where the option to invest itself is sold to realise value.

Projects move from being less attractive propositions to bankable investments with favorable developments which could include increases in price or production volumes, tax holidays or lower capital requirements from improved technologies. The real options framework provides the analyst with the platform to incorporate such later day enhancements into today's decision making.

For the wind turbine acquisition project discussed in earlier chapters, several embedded options could help reverse the investment decision. For instance, the availability of a more efficient turbine generating a higher output, higher offtake prices for the power so generated, the provision of tax breaks and accelerated write-down allowances etc. could favorably alter the project's profile.

Value from Wait and Watch Options

The option to postpone an investment could prove valuable when additional information viz., prices, market demand, costs etc., could increase the worth and / or reduce the risks associated with a given project. This option is observed most frequently in resource extraction industries such as mining, which are exposed to volatile commodity prices. Having secured a mining lease, the company has the option to operate the mine when ruling prices are high while it could be shut down when prices tank.

The decision to delay an investment could also be determined by external factors such as prevailing market interest rates. If sponsors perceive a significant probability that rates may drop, a project that is not acceptable today could be viable at a later date, at a lower cost of funds.

In addition to reducing the risk in multi-stage projects, the decision tree analysis could potentially add value to projects by tying expenditures closely to the maturation of a given opportunity. For instance splitting one market research investment into two smaller (possibly even adding up to more than the initially proposed budget) enables the sponsor to allocate resources more appropriately, (D'Souza, 2002).

The Costs of Wait and Watch Options

In certain situations, the option to expand production could involve duplication of expenditure or scrapping some of the existing infrastructure in favor of larger facilities, which are the costs associated with the managerial option to expand. Such losses from the write-off of project assets are viewed as intrinsic costs of holding on to the options in question. Pending changes in regulations which could affect the project adversely, a possible loss of market share or loss of the first-mover advantage to a competitor are all costs associated with investing later rather than sooner.

Conclusion

Real options discussed in this chapter help decision makers reduce risk and thus limit the downside by postponing or abandoning a given project investment. However, real options are different in treatment and valuation from financial options, as the exercise price of real options itself could vary with time. It is generally accepted that management flexibility combined with the opportunities to gather additional information can alter or even reverse an initial decision. While a discounted cash-flow analysis is the logical starting point for project analysis, in several cases, it needs to be strengthened with real option analysis.

References

Bowe, Michael and Lee, Ding Lun 'Project Evaluation in the Presence of Multiple Embedded Real Options: Evidence from the Taiwan High-Speed Rail Project', Journal of Asian Economics, Vol. 15 (1), February 2004, p 71 – 98.

D'Souza, Fabian 'Project Analysis? Climb the Decision Tree', Harvard Business School Working Knowledge, 9 September, 2002.

Knowledge at Wharton, 'Taiwan's High-Speed Rail: It's Been A Rapid Learning Curve' 26 September, 2007, http://www.knowledgeatwharton.com.cn/index.cfm?fa=viewfeature&articleid=1718&languageid=1.

Luehrman, Timothy A. 'Strategy as a Portfolio of Real Options', Harvard Business Review, September – October 1998 p 89 – 99.

Public Private Partnerships and the Role of Governments

KEY CHAPTER CONCEPTS

1. The public-private partnership is structured so as to provide competitive returns to private sector investors while ensuring a higher quality of service which is more cost-efficient compared to purely public sector provision of the same.
2. Government support for private infrastructure initiatives is justified when the social 'spill-over' effects are greater than the project's social costs.
3. Private initiatives also bring about spin-off effects such as the launch of several ancillary services, additional tax revenues to the state and setting the expenditure multiplier in motion.
4. Governments typically offer tax holidays, land on nominal terms and support infrastructure, cash subsidies, loan guarantees and on occasion, equity participation. Such incentives increase the economic attractiveness of otherwise marginal projects.

GLOSSARY OF NEW TERMS

Concession Agreement An agreement between the host government and the project company to permit construction and operation of a project.

Contingent Liability Defined obligations payable subject to certain events and under certain future circumstances.

Public-Private Partnership Private sector participation in traditionally public sector domains such as infrastructure creation and service provision.

Government Guarantee A contingent liability assumed by the government to encourage investments, reduce project risks and hence project costs.

Moral Hazard A tendency for a party to be less careful, because it is insulated from risk or shares a part of the risk with an external agency.

Train to Fly: The Sydney Airport Link

The 10 km two-track underground railway between Sydney Kingsford Smith Airport and Sydney Central Station was completed in May 2000. The Airport Link Company (ALC), the special purpose vehicle undertaking the 30 year BOOT contract was to design, construct and operate the tracks, tunnels and four new stations project. The sponsors infused $ 30m in equity while the National Australia Bank contributed $190m in debt. The state government financed $700m towards the construction of the rail link[*].

The airport link approval process was complex as the line passed through five local government areas and the airport, which was located in the Commonwealth territory, administered by the Federal Airports Commission. The government State Rail Authority (SRA) assumed all approval risks. Further, at the design stage, the SRA also shouldered the risks associated with delays or costs in dealing with the Federal Airports Commission. SRA also undertook to acquire the

---

[*]   *Based on Ng and Loosemore (2007)*

(*Continued*)

land along the route and for the stations, including ensuring access to the sites. For two stations at the airport, and tunnel lengths, the SRA executed a separate agreement with the Federal Airports Commission. Finally, the SRA assumed risk of *force majeure* and of general industrial disputes challenging government policy.

Project related risks such as underground track design risk was borne by ALC. During the construction phase, ALC was responsible for the construction risk, having to deliver the stations, tracks, tunnels and associated infrastructure on time, within budget and conforming to agreed quality standards. While maintenance of the infrastructure and facilities was left to ALC, the SRA absorbed the risk of operating trains, selling tickets, meeting service standards and most importantly, risks associated with government policies having a direct or indirect impact on the use of the rail link. ALC hedged the risk from floating interest rate debt to help fix its interest payout liabilities. A significant portion of the project expenditure was denominated in local currency. However, ALC was to carry the market / revenue risk over the concession period, since revenue was directly dependent on level of train usage. The SRA capped this risk by agreeing to compensate ALC if passenger traffic fell below the expected 48,000 trips per day. The SRA, acting as an arm of the government, had predicted that this was relatively low risk, as models indicated traffic volumes of 68,000 per day by 2013.

Soon it became apparent that the SRA had underestimated the risks involved and that ALC was protected from the downside risk owing to the structure of the revenue share and compensation agreement. A taxi ride from the airport to the city center was found to be cheaper and more convenient. Threats from terrorist attacks and the collapse of Ansett Airlines, the second largest operator, aggravated the situation. Consequently, 6 months after launching the service, passenger volumes stood at 12,000 as against the 46,000 initially projected. The government offered concession fares to groups and offered combined airline and train ticket packages. Soon, the state government also shut down the airport link bus service to force people onto the train. As of 2006, traffic volumes have been less that

(*Continued*)

30% of forecast levels and the government has continued to compensate ALC for the shortfall. This is partly because the fares on the link line are much higher than comparable alternative modes.

Clearly, revenue and usage patterns for large public infrastructure projects cannot be predicted for decades in advance. Risks involved in such projects need to be thoroughly analyzed and appropriately managed. Community involvement in the planning process and encouragement to use the facilities provided are key. Residual risks are best borne by governments but such costs need to be commensurate with the social benefits delivered by privately implemented projects.

Introduction

Public infrastructure services have traditionally been provided by governments, where select project assets are procured from the private sector. More recently, owing to fiscal constraints and driven by the need to increase efficiencies, such services are provided by private entrepreneurs under specified terms and subject to governmental oversight.

Government involvement in projects remains all pervasive. Typically, private infrastructure projects mandate large amounts of irreversible capital investments with long maturities, are regulated by governments and the services provided are deemed essential by society. "The presence of the government as mitigator of risk may be a necessary condition since the control of many of the variables that affect important aspects of the project are under its responsibility, such as interest rates, regulation and others, because market risk is such that the project is not feasible from the perspective of the private investor[¶]."

Involving governments as stakeholders helps align the interests of sovereign and provincial governments with private entrepreneurs ensuring that the projects are not subject to undue pressures and opportunist

---

¶   *Brandao and Saraiva (2007)*

behavior by the governments and consequently, reduces project risk. While guaranteeing project debt, however governments require to balance between the contingent liabilities assumed and maximising returns to society. This chapter deals with the role played by governments and government agencies in guaranteeing project debt, as equity investors and as clients procuring the service sought to be delivered by the project.

Scope for Government Interface in Projects

The public sector has traditionally financed and managed infrastructure assets. Host governments for most part have lead the development of primary energy and energy-related projects and more recently, have employed limited recourse structures to finance infrastructure development as well, (Pollio, 1998). In recent times, the private sector has demonstrated interest in taking over the responsibilities of financing constructing and operating infrastructure assets. Governments have favored such moves owing to fiscal constraints and the need for greater efficiencies. Japan, for instance, introduced the private finance initiative (PFI) in 1999 to encourage private sector participation in infrastructure provision. Kleiss and Imura (2006) have analysed municipal solid waste incineration plants built under the PFI and observe that a consistent legislative framework goes a long way in helping deliver the anticipated benefits from such initiatives.

Expropriation / Nationalisation, currency convertibility and transferability are all under government control and legally enforceable assurances from the governments would be required prior to committing investments. However, assurances regarding the consistency of the regulatory environment tend to be less reliable. Governments could be tempted to increase taxes or to suspend tax holidays, or be compelled to impose stricter environmental compliance standards once the investment is made. The concession agreements should provide for adequate compensation to ensure that such regulatory changes do not adversely impact the project's prospects.

Government Guarantees

By definition project companies take on large quantities of debt, backed by the project assets. However, given the asset specificity and the limited ability to enforce security interests, lenders (or a syndicate) could be reluctant to lend to projects, especially in weaker economies. Alternatively, the consortium of lenders could choose to impose a risk premium on the project, thereby pushing costs up. Under such circumstances, sovereign or provincial governments could step in to guarantee the project debt, thereby imposing a contingent liability on tax payer money. In other words, if the project defaults on its debt service, the host government takes on the responsibility of making good such defaults to the lenders, within specified limits.

The private sector has demonstrated the competence to execute projects more efficiently and thereby bringing down the overall costs. However, the higher costs of borrowing compared to the public sector increase project costs. Government guarantees could ensure availability of debt funding for the project, while also helping lower the cost of borrowing, and while retaining the efficiency brought in by the private partner. The public and private partners determine their exposure (immediate or contingent) to the project, striking a balance, between the higher outlays on construction for public sector projects and the higher cost of capital for the private investor.

An analyst cannot overlook the fact that governments should not assume the risk of project failure, for instance, by guaranteeing demand for the services to be provided, in which case, the private partners have little incentive to optimise project designs and to operate the projects efficiently. Such guarantees could end up being open-ended as in the case discussed at the beginning of the chapter and could impose disproportionate costs on the tax payers. Conversely, private participants might consider the project too risky to be undertaken in the absence of such guarantees.

Generally, projects operating in a monopoly set-up require guarantees on offtake and tariffs charged, while those operating in a competitive environment are unlikely to insist on guarantees. In countries where government controlled utilities continue to distribute electric power, private sector power producers insist on government guarantees, especially when the solvency of the utilities is suspect. For airport, road and bridge projects, revenue guarantees could be substituted by monopoly assurances that the government would not allow the development of competitor facilities that could impact project revenues.

The optimal level of project risk is therefore, ultimately determined by the capital structure. When the project company's shareholders have a large equity stake in the new project, both parties – the guarantor and the borrower - gain by choosing a low risk project for long maturity debts. This helps blend the respective strengths of the public and private partners, minimising project costs and maximising social and economic returns.

Agency Problems and Moral Hazard in Providing Guarantees

Some analysts have observed that the provision of such guarantees induces a moral hazard, wherein project managers assume risks they would otherwise not have accepted. Angoua, Lai and Soumare (2008) highlight the increase in a firm's risk appetite when its project debt is guaranteed. Further, the authors discuss the moral hazard and divergence in incentives between the guarantor and the borrower[**]. Project sponsors tend to assume greater risks when their own stakes in the project are relatively small. According to Farrell (2003), the possibility of encountering agency problems in project finance structures rises with the increasing number of stakeholders. The project activity is obscured from the scrutiny of appropriate principals with the involvement of too many supervisors. Due to such lack of transparency some of the project's wealth could be transferred to management or large shareholders at the cost of smaller shareholders or external guarantors of debt.

[**] *This could be true of any insurance provision: in this case, it is presumed that the government is not as adept at risk appraisal and management as a professional insurance company.*

Others argue that even if governments play a part in exchange rate determination, the risks associated with interest rate and exchange rate movements should ideally be borne by the private partners. This eliminates the tendency to take large speculative open positions in currencies and debt with floating interest rates, (Thobani, 1999).

Government Equity

A key argument in favor of public-private partnerships is the capacity available with the private partner, leading to innovative approaches to project design and implementation and more significantly, the transfer of know-how from the private to the public partner. Government equity ownership through public agencies provides adequate control on project operations to ensure that social objectives and superior quality of services are not sacrificed in the quest for private profits. "To be attractive and viable, the shareholding structure of the SPV (Special Purpose Vehicle) should secure the interest of both the public and private partner, namely providing enough public capital and sufficient private sector know-how," (Moszoro and Gasiorowski, 2008).

Most infrastructure services including power, water, airports, telecom, etc., have been deemed 'natural' monopolies, and have, traditionally been owned and operated by governments. Recent advances in project finance and reform measures initiated in several countries have witnessed increased private sector involvement in the provision of such services. Except for telecom, most other services are generally continue to be provided by monopoly service providers. In the absence of a sizable government equity ownership[††] (of the order of 26% of the paidup capital), it is feared that a public sector monopoly could be replaced by a private sector monopoly, with sufficiently large rent-seeking opportunities. In the

---

[††]   *Generally referred to as a "blocking minority', and defined by the Company Law in vogue, a certain percentage ownership and voting rights are required to ensure that the smaller shareholder has the 'voice' to block unfavorable decisions proposed by the larger shareholder(s). According to the Indian Companies Act, for instance, a company's board requires 75% votes to pass "special resolutions" i.e., to implement major decisions and 25%+ shareholding is normally considered a "blocking minority".*

absence of water-tight concession agreements, effective regulation by public agencies and efficient legal enforcement systems, there is little that prevents a benchmark sector monopoly service provider from resorting to unreasonable pricing. Having the government as a significant shareholder is expected to eliminate such tendencies.

Government Risk

Despite the advantages discussed above, government equity holding is accompanied by definite disadvantages to the project, and under certain circumstances, could destroy shareholder value as well. The prices for the infrastructure services provided are regulated by appropriately qualified statutory agencies. However, if a democratically elected government is seen as a part owner and hence a service provider, the project company could be subject to political pressures to keep prices low. Under extreme conditions, the government as owner, regulator and manager rolled into one, could compel project companies to sell product below cost. This has been witnessed in the case of the Indian public sector oil marketing companies engaged in refining and selling petrol, diesel, LPG cooking gas and kerosene. Raising the retail prices of the distillates in tandem with rising international crude oil prices has proved politically unpalatable. Such compulsions are referred to as 'government risk' and markets tend to account for the possibility that government ownership could depress profitability of the companies concerned.

Dastidar, Fisman and Khanna (2007) quantify the risks of government ownership and management in the Indian context. The authors observe that the defeat of a pro-reform coalition in the general elections in 2004 and the unexpected entry of a relatively conservative government led to a sudden and significant drop in the market valuation of firms slated for privatisation. Government controlled companies that were definitely in the line for privatization lost 3.5% relative to *comparator* firms, given the possibility that the proposed privatization could be put on hold. More noteworthy is the observation that government controlled firms that were merely candidates being evaluated for eventual privatization fell 7.5% relative to private firms. This clearly implies that the market places a premium for companies under private management while discounts those with government ownership. In other words, the intertwining of the political pressures and economic objectives leads to sub-optimal outcomes, and to value-destruction of sizable proportions.

Conclusion

Governments play a major part in projects as equity holders, lenders, guarantors, regulators, facilitators and even as customers in some cases. Government participation brings benefits to projects by assuming risks it can control viz., regulatory risks and more importantly, by *not* assuming risks it cannot control viz., project patronage / revenue risks. The risk allocation matrix by Grimsey and Lewis (2004), annexed to this chapter, could serve as a guide. The first step in optimizing government involvement and in cutting out adverse impacts is to identify all guarantees and estimating the values of the contingent liabilities thus assumed. Doing so presents a clear picture of the costs and risks of the guarantees provided, rather than when the government actually has to pay up. Governments should then be mandated to make budgetary provisions for eventual payouts against such contracted liabilities, much as banks provide for eventual defaults on outstanding loans. Above all, stable macroeconomic policies and effective enforcement of property rights help reduce risks and encourage private sector investment in the country.

References

Angoua, Paul; Lai, Van Son and Soumare, Issouf 'Project Risk Choices Under Privately Guaranteed Debt Financing', *The Quarterly Review of Economics and Finance*, Vol. 48, No. 1, 2008, p 123 – 152.

Brandao, Luiz E T and Saraiva, Eduardo C G, 'Valuing Government Guarantees in Toll Road Projects', March 2007, www.realoptions.org.

Dastidar, Siddhartha G. Fisman, Raymond and Khanna, Tarun 'Testing Limits to Policy Reversal: Evidence from Indian Privatizations', NBER Working Paper No. 13427, National Bureau of Economic Research, USA.

Farrell, L M 'Principal – agency Risk in Project Finance', *Internal Journal of Project Management*, Vol. 21, No. 8, November 2003, p 547 – 561.

Grimsey D, and Lewis Mervyn (2004) Public Private Partnerships, Cheltman, UK: Edward Elgar.

Kleiss, Torsten and Imura, Hidefumi 'The Japanese Private Finance Initiative and its Application in the Municipal Solid Waste Management Sector', *International Journal of Project Management*, Vol. 24, No.7, 2006, p 614 – 621.

Moszoro, Marian and Gasiorowski, Pawel 'Optimal Capital Structure of Public-Private Partnerships', IMF Working Paper No. 08 /1, International Monetary Fund, January 2008.

Ng, A. and Loosemore Martin 'Risk Allocation in the Private Provision of Public Infrastructure, *International Journal of Project Management*, Vol. 25, 2007 p 66 – 76.

Pollio, Gerald, 'Project Finance and International Energy Development', *Energy Policy*, Vol. 26, No. 9, August 1998, p 687 – 697.

Thobani, Mateen 'Private Infrastructure, Public Risk', Finance & Development, March 1999, p 50 – 53.

Appendix A: Risk Matrix for Public Sector / Private Sector of Infrastructure Investments (Source: Grimsey and Lewis, 2004)

Type of Risk	Source of Risk	Risk Taken By
Site Risks		
Site conditions	Ground conditions, supporting structures	Construction contractor
Site preparation	Site redemption, tenure, pollution/ discharge, obtaining permits, community liaison	Operating company / Project company
	Pre-existing liability	Government
Land use	Native title, cultural heritage	Government
Technical Risks		
	Fault in tender specifications	Government
	Contractor design fault	Design contractor
Construction Risks		
Cost overrun	Inefficient work practices and wastage of materials	Construction contractor
	Changes in law, delays in approval etc.	Project company / investors
Delay in completion	Lack of coordination of contractors, failure to obtain standard planning approvals	Construction contractor
	Insured *force majeure* events	Insurer
Failure to meet performance criteria	Quality shortfall / defects in construction / commissioning tests failure	Construction contractor / project company

(Continued)

Appendix A: (Cont'd)

Type of Risk	Source of Risk	Risk Taken By
Operating Risks		
Operating cost overrun	Project company request or change in practice	Project company / investors
	Industrial relations, repairs, occupational health and safety, maintenance, other costs	Operator
	Government change to output specifications	Government
Delays or interruption in operation	Operator fault	Operator
	Government delays in granting or renewing approvals pending contracted inputs	Government
Shortfall in service quality	Operator fault	Operator
	Project company fault	Project company / investors
Revenue Risks		
Increase in input prices	Contractual violations by government-owned support network	Government
	Contractual violations by private supplier	Private supplier
	Other	Project company / investors
Changes in taxes, tariffs	Fall in revenue	Project company / investors
Demand for output	Decreased demand	Project company / investors

(Continued)

Appendix A: (Cont'd)

Type of Risk	Source of Risk	Risk Taken By
Financial Risks		
Interest rates	Fluctuations in insufficient hedging	Project company / government
Inflation	Payments eroded by inflation	Project company / government
Force majeure risk	Floods, earthquakes, riots, strikes	Shared
Regulatory / Political Risks		
Changes in law	Construction period	Construction contractor
	Operating period	Project company, with government compensation as per contract
Political interference	Breach / cancellation of licence	Government
	Expropriation	Insurer, project company / investor
	Failure to renew approvals, discriminatory taxes, import restrictions	Government
Project Default Risks		
	Combination of risks	Equity investors followed by banks, bondholders and institutional lenders
	Sponsor suitability risk	Government
Asset Risks		
	Technical obsolescence	Project company
	Termination	Project company / operator
	Residual transfer value	Government, with compensation for maintenance obligation

CASE STUDIES

The Panama Canal: At the Cross Roads

Case Study in Financial Modeling and Sensitivity Analyses

"Panama is betting on its future"
—*President Martin Torrijos, 2006*

"The Canal is the country's main economic activity"
—*Panama Canal Authority, 2006.*

Introduction

The referrendum approving the expansion of the Panama Canal is hailed the most significant Panamanian decision ever: "the foundation to build a better country"[1]. The Panama Canal as we know it was completed in the year 1914 and despite ongoing maintenance and periodic upgrades, is not sized to accommodate the largest modern day ocean-going cargo vessels. The proposed expansion includes the provision of new sets of locks, 40% longer and 60% wider than the existing ones: one each at the Pacific and Atlantic sides of the Canal. Consequently, the expansion project is formally referred to as the "third set of locks project". The project also includes excavation of new access channels to the new locks and proposes to widen and deepen the existing navigational channels[2]. The navigation channels are to be deepened while the maximum operating level of the Gatun Lake is to be raised. Annexure 1 to this case lays out the plan and the elevation levels of the Canal.

The US\$ 5.25 billion (US\$ 5250 million) project is expected to be completed in 2014, exactly a century after the original canal was commissioned. The details of cost estimates are provided in annexure 2 to this case[3]. The expansion is slated to make the canal more productive, efficient and safe and the increased toll from ships using the canal is expected to pay for the expansion: the canal expansion project is expected to create a "self liquidating asset". In addition, the incremental revenues generated would flow to the treasury, towards funding public expenditure.

---

[1]   *President Martin Torrijos, quoted in "Panamanians Back Canal Expansion", BBC News, http:// news.bbc.co.uk/2/hi/americas/6074106.stm*

[2]   *http://www.pancanal.com/eng/expansion/index.html*

[3]   Annexures 2–6: Proposal for the Panama Canal Expansion Project prepared by ACP, 24 April 2006.

The government is also faced with a policy dilemma: hoping to spend its way to higher real incomes to compensate for a slowing economy, while faced with the Panamanian economy's limited capacity to accommodate additional stimulus without aggrevating inflationary pressures[4]. According to some estimates, some 60% of Panama's three million citizens live in extreme poverty and doubling the canal's capacity and consequent revenue streams are expected to help lift large sections out of poverty. Annexure 3 provides information on Panama's macroeconomic parameters, projected through 2013.

Background

The Panama Canal currently accounts for 5% of all world shipping, or about 14,000 transits a year. The 50 mile (80 km) long canal presently employs 8000 Panamanians and is a great source of national pride and foreign currency. However, demand has progressively outstripped available capacity, with ships having to wait in queue to pass through. Some of the larger ships carrying oil, grain and other container cargo are presently unable to use the inter-oceanic canal.

The Panama Canal is a national asset of the Republic of Panama, which may not be "sold, assigned, mortgaged or otherwise encumbered or transferred" and the Panama Canal Authority (ACP) is charged with the fundamental mission of ensuring that the Canal is preserved for "peaceful and uninterrupted service of the maritime community, international trade and the Republic of Panama." The ACP is created under a special statute, as an entity of the Government of Panama and is exclusively in charge of operation, maintenance, administration, preservation, and modernization of the Panama Canal[5].

---

[4]   The Economist Intelligence Unit, "The Pain in Panama", 24 July 2008.

[5]   Overview of the ACP at http://www.pancanal.com/eng/general/acp-overview.html

History of the Expansion Project

Efforts aimed at enhancing canal capacity were initiated back in 1939 by the United States, albeit with a view to enabling the passage of war ships whose dimensions exceeded the size of the existing locks. The outbreak of World War II compelled the suspension of construction activity after significant advances in excavation for the third set of locks. In the 1980s, a commission comprising members from Panama, Japan and the United States determined that larger lock chambers and the addition of a third set of locks are the best solutions to address the constraints imposed by the canal's imited capacity. This has been reaffirmed by the studies instituted by the Panama Canal Authority. In order to optimize construction time and costs, the new locks would overlap with large portions of the area excavated by the United States in the 1930s. The new locks would be connected to the existing channel system through new navigation channels.

Market Risk

Sceptics of the expansion project point out that the growth in container traffic has largely been triggered by the emergence of China as an exporter and the increased volume of US imports from the East, including China. The trade imbalance between China and the United States, observed at the time of preparing the financial projections for the expansion project, is clearly unsustainable and as domestic consumption in the United States slows down, China would need to look for other export markets or to increase consumption at home, to reduce its dependence on exports. Enthusiasts argue that a slow down in US spending would actually lead to larger volumes of imports of low-priced goods from China and other Asian economies and therefore would strengthen the case for the expansion project. Besides, the discovery of large oil reserves in Brazil and potential for export of ethanol and other minerals from Latin American countries to China, India etc., could also boost traffic volumes through the canal.

Rival Links

The ACP had earlier warned that if measures were not taken immediately, business would be lost to altenative shipping routes. Panama's northern neighbour, Nicaragua has proposed to resurrect plans to construct a canal between the Pacific and Atlantic oceans[6].

A survey conducted way back in the 1830s suggested that the inter-oceanic link through Nicaragua would follow the San Juan River from the Atlantic Ocean to Lake Nicaragua and then through a series of locks and tunnels to the Pacific Ocean, with a total length of 172 miles (278 km). However, basing on an erroneous picture on a 10 cent Nicaraguan postage stamp, concerns relating to the volcanic activity of mount Momotombo and consequent seismic activity were raised, even as it was at least 100 miles from the proposed canal route. The realization of the dream is fraught with uncertainty as it is slated to cost in excess of $25 billion, consume at least 12 years to complete and is likely to adversely impact rivers and forests in its wake. Nevertheless, if and when the canal is built through Nicaragua, it is bound to challenge the Panama canal's monopoly on inter-oceanic transportation. "Dry canal" rivals to link the two oceans, including high-speed railway lines and modern roads are unlikely to pose a serious threat to the viability of the expanded canal[7]. The routing of the US inter-modal route, considered a viable alternative, partly running

---

[6] "Panamanians Back Canal Expansion", BBC News, 23rd October, 2006.
[7] "A Man, A Plan, A Canal – Panama?", The Economist, 26th September, 1998.

on land to reach the US east-coast from North-Eastern Asia is shown in Annexure 4.

Environmental Concerns

The proposed expansion project does not require bringing additional area under the management of the ACP. The project does not entail the relocation communities or settlements. The enlargement does not involve the inundation of forests, reserved or otherwise, or archeological, agricultural, industrial or tourist sites. Feasibility studies have also observed that the project would not harm water or air quality in the area, and the lock design is expected to make efficient use of water available. ANCON, the National Association for Nature Conservation has confirmed that the water saving basins and the third lock would contribute very low levels of salinity to the waters of the Gatun Lake and at these levels, the biologic separation of the oceans would be preserved. While keeping the biodiversity intact, the water in the lake would remain suitable for human consumption[8]. Disposal of debris from excavation is unlikely to pose major disruptions.

Inputs to the Financial Model

The expansion of the canal is mandated by the growing demand from traffic – larger number of voyages by larger ships – and the enlarged canal is slated to be sized to play a significant role for the next century or so. Yet, projections beyond 2025, i.e. beyond the first ten years of canal operations would involve significant conjecture and hence even as the canal is expected to have a useful life in excess of 50 years before requiring major upgrades, vessel size and cargo volume are assumed to

---

[8] http://www.ancon.org/mambo/index.php?option=com_content&task=view&id=117&Itemid=150

stabilize at 2025 levels, to provide for a conservative basis for revenue estimates[9].

- While the current transit capacity is being fully exploited, the enlarged capacity is likely to come on stream in 2014. It is estimated that a total of 5300 ocean-going vessels would be in business in 2010[10], growing from then on at 5% per annum over the previous year's number. A weekly containership service between Northeast Asia and the U.S. East Coast using the Suez Canal requires 11 vessels, depending on the number of scheduled port calls. For the Panama Canal, this same service requires 8 vessels. This means that on the Suez route each vessel will make 4.7 round trips per year, with a round trip travel time of 77 days. Through the Panama Canal, each vessel will make 6.5 round trips per year, with a 56 day round trip travel time. This indicates that the Panama Canal offers an important advantage in terms of vessel productivity, so long as the vessels used have similar capacities[11]. Annexures 5, 6 and 7 contain the projections for cargo capacity shipped through the canal and the resulting financial projections.

- Each ocean-going vessel is expected to complete one trip (from origin to destination) per 2 weeks, on average. An estimated 12% of these voyages are expected to take the vessels through the canal in 2014 ("transits"). Each year, an additional 0.5% of voyages are likely to utilize the enlarged canal, reaching an aggregate 14% of all voyages in 2018 and remaining stable thereafter[12].

- Each of the 14,000 transits in 2007 carried an average 20,000 PCUMS[13] tons of cargo; volumes are expected to remain stable for

---

9   Author's estimates where references are not cited.
10   "Maxing Out: Container Ships", The Economist, 1st March, 2007.
11   Panama Canal Expansion proposal page 21 of 70.
12   Author's projections.
13   Panama Canal Universal Measurement System ton = 100 cubic feet of cargo space.

the existing canal. With the enlarged capacity, commencing 2014, cargo tonnage *per voyage* is projected to grow at 3% each year over the previous year's tonnage, for the next decade and stabilize thereafter.

• The transit tariff charged per PCUMS ton has been US$ 4.0 in 2007, growing at a steady 2% per annum in the absence of the expansion. The expanded capacity is likely to enhance ACP's pricing power[14]. Commencing 2014, transit tariff is slated to be raised at 3.7% per annum over the previous year's tariff, so as to double the tariff over 20 years. Tariffs could be expected to grow at 2% per annum beyond 2035.

• Panama is said to have the most comprehensive wildlife management systems in Central America, through the 15 national parks and reserves covering over 29% of the territory. The government is keen to encourage ecotourism to benefit from the presence of 933 bird species and 10,000 plant varieties – more than the total of North America and Europe combined. Foreign and domestic tourism is worth about US$ 300 million per year[15]. The enlarged canal is expected to be a destination for tourists, generating incremental revenues from tourism and support services to the tune of almost US$ 30 million per annum, though such estimates are routinely ignored while preparing the base-case assumptions.

• Incremental operating expenses are estimated at 8% of (incremental) project revenues for 2014, growing from then on at 2% over the previous year's expenditure. ACP does not anticipate expanding its administrative set-up but US$ 15 m of administrative expenditure is to be allocated to the expansion project.

---

14   "It's Going to Cost More to Ship Through the Panama Canal", Logistics Today, May 2007, p 12.
15   http://www.nationsencyclopedia.com/economies/Americas/Panama.html

- The enlarged canal is expected to have a useful life of 50 years, after which it would have to be renovated and upgraded.

Issues for Discussion

The ACP estimates that the project would have a simple payback of about ten years and that project debt could be repaid in 8 years of operations. Project Analysts are required to independently confirm the financial viability of the expansion project.

- Assuming that the canal (expansion) project is all equity financed, and that the applicable tax rate is 20%, the analyst should draw up the profit and loss account and the cash-flow statement for the first twenty years of operations (2014 – 2035) in US$ million.

- Taking a cue from the payback period for the project, the analyst should weigh possibilities for the optimal capital structure for the project if:

  a. the parallel canal is built in Nicaragua.

  b. the parallel canal is *not* built in Nicaragua.

- The financial model is to be developed, generating among other things, the debt amortization schedule, assuming that:

  (i) the Debt required is $2.3 billion drawn in equal installments in 2010 and 2011.

  (ii) ten year fixed rate US$ denominated debt is available at 9.5% per annum.

  (iii) the equity holders' expectation from the project is 18% per annum.

- Given the inputs provided, a detailed sensitivity analysis would reveal the risk variables to which the financial model is most sensitive.

- The best case and worst case scenarios are to be built by arriving at best guess estimates for the range of values for each of the risk variables.

- Non-financial risks embedded in the project design are listed and appropriate risk-mitigation measures are designed.

ℰℭ

Annexure 1: Route Plan and Section Showing Levels for the Panama Canal Expansion Project

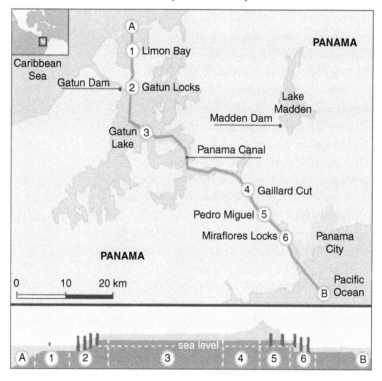

Annexure 2: Cost Estimates for the Panama Canal Expansion Project

Cost estimate for the third set of locks project

Project components	Investment estimate*
New locks	
Atlantic locks	1,110
Pacific locks	1,030
Contingency for new locks**	590
Total for new locks	**2,730**
Water saving basins	
Atlantic water saving basins	270
Pacific water saving basins	210
Contingency for water saving basins**	140
Total for water saving basins	**620**
Access channels for new locks	
Atlantic access channels (dredging)	70
Pacific access channels (dry excavation)	400
Pacific access channels (dredging)	180
Contingency for access channels**	170
Total for new locks access channels	**820**
Existing navigational channel improvements	
Deepening and widening of atlantic entrance	30
Widening of the gatun lake channels	90
Deepening and widening of pacific entrance	120
Contingency for existing channel improvements**	50
Total for navigational channel improvements	**290**
Water supply improvements	
Increase the maximum level of gatun lake to 27.1 m (89') PLD	30
Deepening of the navigational channels to 9.1 m (30')PLD	150
Contingency for water supply improvements**	80
Total for water supply improvements	**260**
Inflation during the construction period*	**530**
Total investment	**5,250 M***

*Millions of balboas, rounded to the nearest tenths
**The contingency includes possible variations for each component
***Assumes a general inflation of 2% per year above what is included in the contingency

Annexure 3: Panama Macro-Economic Parameters, projections through 2013 (in shaded cells)

Subject Descriptor	Units	2006	2007	2008	2009	2010	2011	2012	2013	Series-specific Notes
Gross domestic product, constant prices	National currency (billion)	15.256	16.965	18.271	19.587	21.075	22.656	24.242	25.817	Gross domestic product at constant market prices Source: National Statistical Office Latest actual data: 2007 Base Year: 1996 Use of chain weighted prices indices: No Notes: In 2004, the authorities released major revisions to their constant price GDP data from 1996, and introduced demand side accounts for the first time.

Gross domestic product, constant prices	Annual percent change	8.652	11.2	7.7	7.2	7.6	7.5	7	6.5	Primary domestic currency: U.S. dollars Data last updated: 03/2008 Gross domestic product, constant prices (National currency).
Inflation, average consumer prices	Index, 2000 = 100	107.92	112.412	120.73	126.646	131.585	136.717	142.186	147.873	Consumer price index annual average Source: National Statistical Office Latest actual data: 2007 Primary domestic currency: U.S. dollars Data Last updated: 03/2008

(Continued)

Annexure 3: (Cont'd)

Subject Descriptor	Units	2006	2007	2008	2009	2010	2011	2012	2013	Series-specific Notes
Inflation, average consumer prices	Annual percent change	2.462	4.162	7.4	4.9	3.9	3.9	4	4	Inflation, average consumer prices (Index, 2000 = 100).
Population	Persons (million)	3.284	3.343	3.403	3.465	3.527	3.591	3.655	3.655	Population Source: National Statistical Office Latest actual data: 2000 Primary domestic currency: U.S. dollars Data last updated: 03/2008
Current account balance	U.S. dollars (billion)	−0.552	−1.579	−1.779	−2.527	−3.38	−3.23	−2.514	−1.991	Balance on current transactions excluding exceptional financing

Source: International Monetary Fund, World Economic Outlook Database, April 2008.

| Current account balance | Percent of GDP | −3.222 | −8 | −7.782 | −9.8 | −11.7 | −10 | −7 | −5 |

Source: National Statistical Office

Latest actual data: 2007

Primary domestic currency: U.S. dollars

Data last updated: 03/2008

Gross domestic product, current prices (National currency)

Current account balance (U.S. dollars).

Annexure 4: The US inter-modal route running partly on land and linking North-East Asia to the US East Coast is considered the main rival to the "all water" Panama Canal

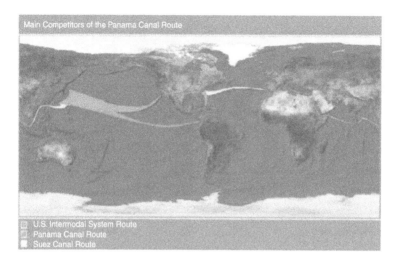

Annexure 5: The post-Panamax vessel has 2.5 times the cargo carrying capacity of the Panamax vessel

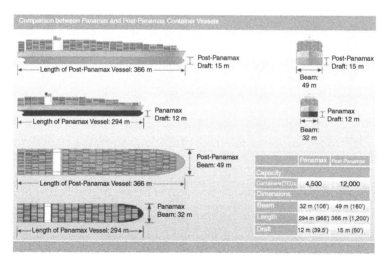

Annexure 6: Growth expected in cargo (tonnage) shipped through the Enlarged Canal

Comparison of tonnage growth per segment

PCUMS tons per market segment'	Year 2005	Year 2025 Canal without an expansion	Year 2025 Canal with an expansion
Containers	98	185	296
Dry bulk	55	49	73
Liquid bulk	34	19	28
Passenger	10	13	19
Car carrier	36	40	58
Refrigerated cargo	19	15	22
General cargo	7	3	4
Others	20	6	8
Total PCUMS tons	**279**	**330**	**508**

'Millions of PCUMS tons

Annexure 7: Summary financial projections for the enlarged canal

Summary of the expanded canal's financial results

Financial results[1]	Year 2005	Year 2025	Aunual average growth rate
PCUMS tons[2]	279	508	3.0%
Transit revenue	1,117	6,101	8.9%
Other revenues	92	125	1.5%
Total revenues	**1,209**	**6,227**	**8.5%**
Operating costs	444	1,016	4.2%
Fee per net ton[3]	218	668	6.5%
Public services fees[3]	2	2	0.0%
Depreciation	61	231	6.8%
Net income	**484**	**4,310**	**11.6%**

[1]Numbers in millions of dollars, including a general inflation of 2% unless indicated otherwise
[2]Millions of PCUMS tons
[3]In order to faciltate comparison, the payments of right per net ton and rate for public services of FY 2006 were adjusted to reflect the change in calculation that applies to FY 2006

Cross Border Project: Lafarge Surma Cement Limited

Case Study in Risk Assessment and Real Options

"You have employed only 175 persons in India, though you claim to be a multinational. A small tea stall in India employs five persons."

—*Bench of the Supreme Court of India, November 2007*

Introduction

"An integrated, dry process cement plant will be built on the north-west bank of the Surma River at Chhatak, Sylhet district, in the far north-east corner of Bangladesh very close to the border with the Indian state of Meghalaya. There are no cement grade deposits of limestone in Bangladesh but it is in plentiful supply in Meghalaya. Thus a limestone quarrying and crushing operation will be established in Meghalaya to serve the cement plant and the two centres of operations will be connected by an overhead belt conveyor[1]."

Background

Lafarge of France is among the world's largest cement manufacturers with operations spread over several countries around the globe, and is

---

[1] *Summary of Project Information, The International Finance Corporation (IFC), 6 May, 1998 http://www.ifc.org/ifcext/spiwebsite1.nsf/1ca07340e47a35cd85256efb00700cee/ 8A9C46FEB1038A2B8525688E00710B60*

slated to contribute the best of technology and managerial practices to the project. The International Finance Corporation (IFC) has demonstrated keen interest in the US$ 255 million project, proposing an 'A' loan of US$ 35 million, 'B' loan of US$ 10 million and equity investment of US$ 10 million. In addition to the direct economic benefits to Bangladesh, spillover benefits such as job creation, skill upgrades and investments into neighboring Meghalaya are viewed positively. Shareholders in Lafarge Surma Cement (LSC), the project company in Bangladesh include the parent, Lafarge of France, the IFC, Cementos Molins of Spain, the Asian Development Bank (ADB), the Islam and Sinha Groups from Bangladesh[2]. Project debt financing has been provided by the IFC, the ADB, the German Development Bank (DEG), the European Investment Bank (EIB), the Netherlands Development Company (FMO) and local Standard Chartered Bank and Arab-Bangladesh Bank.

The strategic logic embedded in project design is compelling. The limestone mines in the remote north eastern Indian state of Meghalaya are otherwise inaccessible. The US$ 20 million investment in Meghalaya was expected to help realize the value of the natural endowment of limestone while contributing to the development of the state. The limestone is transported from the Shella-Nongtrai mine in Meghalaya, India, to the Chhatak plant in

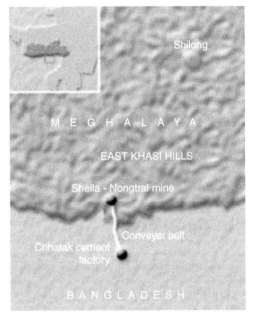

---

[2]   *Project Shareholding is laid out in Annexure 1*

Bangladesh on a 17 km long cross-border conveyor, as shown in the picture alongside[3], 7 km in Indian territory and 10 in Bangladesh. The mining rights and land leases are held by Lum Mawshun Minerals Private Limited, owned by LSC (74%) and by two local Indian tribesmen. Lum Umium Mining Private Limited, a wholly-owned subsidiary of LSC is contracted to carry out the mining operations. Annexure 2 lays out the group holding pattern.

Even as limestone, the main ingredient in cement production is not available in Bangladesh, gypsum, clay, and natural gas are available in abundant measure. Water needed for the manufacturing process is to be pumped from the River Surma, flowing about 200 meters from the project site. The 1.5 million ton per annum plant in Bangladesh would utilize indigenous raw material and imported limestone, combined with upgraded skills of local personnel to produce cement that would meet domestic demand and could possibly be exported. A 30 MW captive power plant provides power to ensure uninterrupted operations of the cement plant. Prior to the commissioning of the LSC plant in 2006, Bangladesh has had to import about 87% of its cement requirement, which in turn, has been exposed to swings in transportation and handling costs. Consequently, government has believed that the unavailability of cement had contributed to the defeciencies in the provision of basic infrastructure in the country.

---

[3] *Picture courtesy: Down to Earth Magazine, Society for Environmental Communications, New Delhi, India, http://www.downtoearth.org.in/full6.asp?foldername=20070815&filename=news&sid=2&page=2&sec_id=4*

Hence, the LSC project which is expected to lower the domestic price of cement substantially, is accorded high priority and is considered to be one of strategic importance by the government of Bangladesh[4].

The High Commissioner of Bangladesh in India and the Foreign Secretary, Government of India, signed the agreement for uninterrupted supply of raw material for the plant. Relevant statutory clearances from the Indian Federal Ministry of Environment & Forests (MoEF), the state government of Meghalaya, the District council and the Chief Conservator of Forests were obtained to facilitate the extraction of limestone from the East Khasi Hills mines in Meghalaya.

Market Risk

An existing plant in Chhatak has an installed capacity of 270,000 tons of cement per annum. Four other plants merely crush clinker imported from India and other countries and bag the cement for the domestic market. The proposed plant would be much larger than all rivals combined and would satisfy a significant portion of domestic demand, currently met by (expensive) imports. LSC, is thus a 'natural' prescription for the prevailing situation. In addition, LSC hopes to supply clinker to the existing crushing units, displacing imported clinker rather than supplanting the units themselves.

Environmental Concerns

The limestone excavation process involves drilling, exploding, crushing, transporting and loading. The rapid environmental impact

---

4   *Summary Environmental Impact Assessment Report, http://www.adb.org/Documents/Environment/ Ban/31911-BAN-SEIA.asp*

assessment[5] points out that there are not archeological or historical sites within a ten km radius of the mine in Meghalaya. The 315 square kilometer area is said to be sparsely populated, with about 60 hamlets and settlements scattered over the hill sides. The report states that "forest is the dominant land use of the region, which is mostly found in the hills. Agriculture is the next important land use in the area. Most agricultural lands are situated in the plain areas located towards southern side of the project site near the international border..... These plantations are interspersed with natural forests and provide a dense vegetal cover to the land[6]." In all, the report confirms that even as no threatened, endangered or rare species of plants are found at the site, the area is home to "rich plant diversity" including old trees, wide variety of medicinal plants, and economically important species. The report goes on to suggest compensatory tree plantation, buffer zone creation, and protection of zones with fragile ecological characteristics, in the event limestone is mined from the hills.

Environmental Impact of Mining in Meghalaya

On visiting the site in May 2006, a former Chief Conservator of Forests, Meghalaya, India, found that about 20 hectares of land that was mined until then was strewn with tree trunks, while the remaining unmined area had stretches of natural forest with tall trees and dense vegetation. This is in sharp contrast to an earlier letter written by a forest officer in the region, which had confirmed that the areas earmarked for mining by the company were not forests as defined by the courts in India[7]. A impact study commissioned by LSC had described the terrain as

---

[5] *Prepared by the Center for Eco-Development, North-Eastern Hill University, Shillong, India, 1997.*

[6] *Rapid EIA report on limestone mining in Meghalaya, page 4, http://www.adb.org/Documents/ Environment/Ban/31911-BAN-SEIA.asp*

[7] *"Meghalaya Limestone Quarries Closed", Down to Earth, Vol. 16, No. 6, August 2007.*

"near wasteland". The Ministry of Environment and Forests (MoEF), Government of India, observed that the forest was being diverted for non-forest activities in violation of relevant court orders, and on the basis of misleading information. The limestone quarries were then shut down, thus starving the LSC plant of vital inputs. The Indian Supreme Court then upheld the closure order and denied LSC permission to transport 600,000 tons of extracted limestone lying at the quaries.

Six months after shutting down plant operations, in November 2007, the expert committees evaluating the merits of the case have advised the Supreme Court to grant *interim* relief under the Forest Conservation Act (1980) and to permit mining subject to conditions, including compulsory reforestation and restoration of affected areas[8]. The objections are said to have been withdrawn in the interest of strengthening bilateral relations between India and Bangladesh[9]. In return, the prosecution has sought to retain sovereignty on the country's limestone reserves and has suggested that Lafarge could set up a cement plant in India, rather than having to transport the input material across the border into Bangladesh. In essence, the MoEF had, at best, sent a mixed signal: on the one hand, hoping to strengthen trade relations with Bangladesh while advocating protectionism on the other. All things considered, LSC might find itself compelled to pay a heavy price just to keep the plant in Bangladesh running, probably including the set-up of a second unit on the Indian side of the border.

Lafarge Surma Cement Limited made a debut on the Dhaka Stock Exchange in November 2003, hoping to mobilize equity capital to complete construction of the cement plant. The 150 million Taka public issue, amounting to about 15.4% of the paid up equity, issued

---

[8]   *Jayantha Mallick, "Lafarge to Resume Meghalaya Mining this Week", Business Line, 27 November, 2007.*

[9]   *"SC Okays Limestone Supply to Lafarge", The Times of India, 24, November, 2007.*

at 100 Taka per share, was oversubscribed by 2.58 times. The summary report of the stock, tracked on the Dhaka Stock Exchange is laid out in Annexure 3. Since receiving the interim relief from the Indian Supreme Court towards end November 2007, the stock has made significant gains from Taka 395 to Taka 639 by September 2008 as shown in Annexure 4.

Mortgage of Indian Territory to Overseas Lenders

Meanwhile, it has also come to light that the mining subsidiaries had acquired 1.232 million square meters of mine land in Meghalaya and had pledged it against the US$ 153 million project loan. While such transfer of rural lands to non-tribals violates the traditional land tenure system, it also falls foul of the applicable statutes, including the Meghalaya Transfer of Land Regulation Act (1971). In the interest of promoting the project the state government of Meghalaya had, in 2001, exempted LSC from the provisions of the Land Transfer Act. However, in response to a petition filed by the tribal land owners, the High Court in Gauhati had restrained LSC from mortgaging additional tribal lands for project loans[10]. Observers question whether an event of default could trigger an enforcement of security interest and could potentially put Indian territory under the control of financial institutions from across the border in Bangladesh.

Issues for Discussion

Evidently, the project benefits from the presence of vital ingredients in close proximity, though on either side of an international border, in a part of the world where joint development of large-scale projects is a

---

[10] *One India News, http://news.oneindia.in/2007/06/19/lafarge-upheld-moef-order-on-lafarge-mining-operations-1182326414.html, 20 June 2007.*

relatively new concept. Project Analysts are required to introspect on the status of the project and on next steps.

- The project has received approvals for each activity from the authorities concerned, in either country. Yet, the interpretation of statutes and definitions of fundamental inputs viz., forest land and economic benefits, have varied over time, especially on the Indian side. Did the project place too much reliance on approvals and leases secured many years prior to the actual implementation? Did planners overlook variations in perspectives at the local, provincial and federal levels?

- Consequently, would it be fair to say that the project remained exposed to government risk? Worse, was the strategic logic itself the undoing of the project?

- The analyst could visualize the project and list the real (strategy) options available to the project.

- Next steps could be decided after considering the value-to-cost metric and the time available to make decisions and to choose courses of action.

- Specific risk-mitigation measures could be debated to counter the government, resource and other non-financial and financial risks faced by the project.

- Would the capital structure need to be revisited in the light of the developments and how could the capital structure help in de-risking the project? Would a larger public shareholding hamper or improve the prospects for the project?

Annexure 1: Project Shareholding Pattern

(Source: Project Summary at http://www.lafarge-bd.com/project_summ.html)

Name of the shareholders	No. of Shares	Holding %	Share capital (Tk)
Surma Holding BV	34,184,955	58.87%	3,418,495,500
International Finance Corporation	5,797,000	9.98%	579,700,000
Asian Development Bank	5,797,000	9.98%	579,700,000
Sinha Fashions Limited	1,755,000	3.02%	175,500,000
Islam Cement Limited	1,595,720	2.75%	159,572,000
Shareholders – Local	8,145,593	14.03%	814,559,300
Shareholders – (NRBs)	793,407	1.37%	79,340,700
Total	58,068,675	100.00%	5,806,867,500

Notes

1. Project Debt: Equity ratio of 60:40

2. US$ 255 million porject cost includes financing charges and upfront working capital

Annexure 2: Group Holding Structure

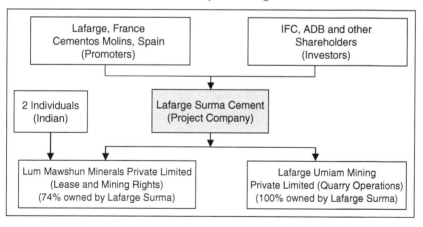

Annexure 3: Snapshot of Lafarge Surma Cement at the Dhaka Stock Exchange as at 2 September 2008

Symbol/Name	Price	Change	% Change	Open	High	Low	Business Segment
LAFSURCEML CATEGORY-Z Lafarge Surma Cement Ltd.	613.25	23.75	4.03	590	615	590	Cement

Volume	Outstanding Cap (mn)	No of Securities	52Wk High	52Wk Low	Face Value	Market Lot
87350	5807.0	58068675	660.00	381.75	100.0	50

Reserve & Surplus (mn)	Market Capital (mn)	Net Turnover (mn)	Net Profit After Tax (mn)	Year End	Half Year End	EPS
−2553.49	3423148.3912	2971.0	414.59	200712	200806	7.14

Electronic Share?	Listing Year	Share Percentage				
		Directorr / Sponsor	Govt.	Institute	Foreign	Public
	2003	78.83	0	5.77	0	15.4

July 17, 2008--As per un-audited half yearly accounts as on 30.06.08, the Company has reported profit after tax of Tk. 414.59 m with EPS of Tk. 7.14 as against last year's half yearly net loss of Tk. (341.91) m and EPS of Tk. (5.89). Accumulated loss of the Company was Tk. (1857.39) m as on 30.06.08.

June 26, 2008--The Company will be placed in "Z" category from existing "G" category with effect from 29.06.08 as the Company has completed two full years from the date of commercial operation as disclosed in the prospectus and has failed to declare dividend as per Regulations.

Annexure 4: Market Analysis: Dhaka Stock Exchange, Bangladesh

Finalcial Performance*

Year	Earning per share	Net Asset Value Per Share	Net Profit After Tax (mn)	Price Earn-ing Ratio	% Dividend	% Dividend Yield
2001	n/a	n/a	n/a	n/a	n/a	n/a
2000	n/a	n/a	n/a	n/a	n/a	n/a
2002	n/a	n/a	n/a	n/a	n/a	n/a
2003	−6.65	93.35	−386.34	-	-	-
2004	−9.13	90.88	−530.13	-	-	-
2005	−8.32	84.82	−483.06	-	-	-
2006	−13.92	68.31	−808.40	-	-	-

Bonus Issue n/a
Right Issue n/a
Last AGM Held: 26/06/2008

Annexure 5: LSC Share price movement on the Dhaka Stock Exchange, Bangladesh, 12 months to September 2008

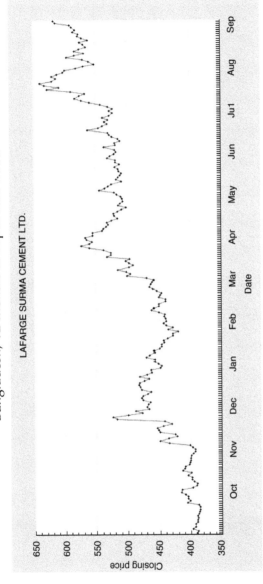

Sound Investments
Comparative Study in Project Opportunities and Growth Options

"…tunnels and bridges are in themselves, uninteresting objects. What should be of interest is the kind of results that they produce, their outcomes, and not the objects themselves"

—*Rothengatter[1] et al., 2002*

A. The Sound Link

Introduction

The 16 km (10 mile) bridge-tunnel *Sound Link* is the longest combined road and rail link in Europe and connects the two metropolitan areas: the Danish capital of Copenhagen and the Swedish city of Malmö. The Øresundsbron (Oresund Bridge or simply the "Sound Bridge") is a combined two-track rail and four-lane road bridge across the Oresund strait. The international European route E20 runs across the bridge and proceeds through the under-sea tunnel. Inaugurated in July 2000, 3 months ahead of schedule, the bridge-tunnel link is one of the largest infrastructure projects in European history[2], while the bridge by itself is the longest 'project financed' border crossing bridge in the world.[3]

---

[1] *Werner Rothengatter, Nils Bruzelius and Bent Flyvbjerg "Big Decisions, Big Risks: Improving Accountability in Mega Projects", Transport Policy, Vol. 9(2), April 2002, p 143–154.*

[2] *Laurence Peter "Scandinavian Mega Bridge Set to Open", BBC News, 30 June 2000.*

[3] *http://en.wikipedia.org/wiki/Oresund_Bridge*

Approximately half the distance between Denmark and Sweden is covered by the bridge, spanning 7.845 km. The bridge ends in the middle of the strait on a 4 km long artificial island, "Peberholm", an unpopulated natural reserve. The Drogden Tunnel which is just over 4 km in length, with about 3.5 km of its length buried under the sea, takes off from the island to reach the Copenhagen Airport.

The link is owned by the Oresund Consortium, in-turn owned by government agencies of the Kingdoms of Sweden and Denmark, the ownership patterns are depicted in annexure 1. The Øresund connection, including the bridge, tunnel, motorway and railway connections on land, was constructed at a total cost of Danish Krone 30.1 billion (~Euro 4.0 billion) in year 2000 prices. The link is expected to pay for itself in about 35 years, i.e. by the year 2035. The useful life of the project is estimated at 100 years. The AAA[4] project bonds are guaranteed jointly by the Kingdoms of Denmark and Sweden and the project is scheduled to repay the debt in about 27 years. Recognizing the potential arising from the link, Sweden has commissioned investments worth Swedish Krona 9.45 billion (~Euro 1.00 billion) more, on the Malmö City Tunnel (2006–2012) as a new rail connection to the bridge.

---

[4]   *Standard & Poors rating.*

Performance

The *Sound link* had carried 1 million drives in the first 75 days, by mid-September 2000, 2 million drives by end-February 2001 and 10 million in three years, by July 2003. The toll rates charged for different categories of vehicles as of January 2008 are listed in Table 1 (discounts of up to 75% are available for regular users). Initially the usage of the bridge was not as high as projected, probably owing to the user charges. However, by 2005, 2006 and thereafter the link has seen a rapid increase in the traffic volumes. This phenomenon may be due to Danes buying homes in Sweden and commuting to work in Denmark, because the price of housing in Malmö is lower than in Copenhagen. In 2007 alone almost 25 million people travelled over the bridge, 15.2 million in cars and buses and 9.6 million by train. Instead of the one-hour ferry trip, commuters are now able to cover the distance in as little as 10 minutes on high-speed trains. The distance is too short for airlines to schedule flights between the two metropolitan areas.

The Oresund waterway had separated the two countries since the last ice age, but the *Sound Link* had brought Scandinavia (Norway, Sweden and Denmark) closer to the European mainland, lifting Copenhagen to a higher position in the European urban hierarchy[5] and boosting trade and jobs in the region as a whole.

While the increased traffic has led to improved financial performance by the link and is slated to shorten the pay-back period for the link by a few years, concerns regarding congestion have emerged. Commuter traffic towards Denmark in the mornings and towards Sweden in the evenings is a cause for concern, with authorities considering improved traffic management measures and investigating possibilities for enhancing link capacity.

---

[5] *Christian Wichmann Matthiessen, "Bridging the Oresund: Potential Regional Dynamics Integration of Copenhagen (Denmark) and Malmo (Sweden): A Cross-Border Project on the European Metropolitan Level", Journal of Transport Geography, Vol. 8(3), September 2000, p 171–180.*

Vehicle Type	Toll (Euro)
Motorcycle	20
Standard car	36
Motorhome/Car + Caravan	71
Minibus (6-9 meters)	71
Bus (longer than 9 meters)	151
Lorry/Truck (longer than 9 meters)	106

Picture: Location and Layout of the Oresund Link showing motorway, bridge and tunnel sections with articificial island

1 Start of four-lane motorway
2 Artificial peninsula at Kastrup
3 4km-long road/rail tunnel
4 Artificial island
5 Road/rail bridge 7.8 km long
6 New 10km road/rail link
7 New coty tunnel (under construction)

Table 1: January 2008 toll for driving the *Sound link* (one way trip)

Environmental Concerns

Activists had expressed concerns that the Link would affect the water and salt flow through the Sound and into and out of the Baltic Sea, would lead to destruction of the cod fishery, and affect other biological systems[6]. An International Expert Panel was constituted to examine and implement strategies to avoid adverse environmental impacts. The expert committee sought to limit sediment discharges to 5% of the dredged material, about 20% of the normal discharge limits for such large-scale projects.

The environment around the link is monitored stringently. Authorities monitor noise levels, rain water run-off from the bridge, emission of carbon dioxide and other

---

[6]   Gray, John S. *"Minimizing Environmental Impacts of a Major Construction: The Øresund Link"*, *Integral Environmental Assessment and Management, Setac Journals, Vol. 2, Issue 2, April 2006.*

greenhouse gases from the traffic, bird collisions in poor visibility conditions etc. An environment report is prepared each year, detailing progress made on each front. By 2002, as many as 28 rare species of plants infrequently found in either country, were discovered on Peberholm. By March 2003, the consortium had engaged actively in restoring the Sound to its pristine state, including providing for nesting boxes for peregrine falcons, offering broad views of the bird's hunting grounds, as shown in the picture alongside. Evidently, the Link was built with little environmental impact and three years after it was completed, environmental conditions have returned to normal.

B. Euro Tunnel

Eurotunnel manages the infrastructure of the ~ Euro 6 billion[7] Channel Tunnel[8] - the under-sea railway link between the UK and France - and operates accompanied truck shuttle and passenger shuttle (car and coach) services between Folkestone, UK and Calais, France. Labeled "the greatest infrastructure success of the 20th century", 37.8 km of the 50 km channel tunnel (comprising two single-track single-direction tunnels and one central service tunnel) are dug at an average of 40 m under the sea bed, making it the longest underwater tunnel in service, anywhere in the world. *Eurotunnel* has received the concession to operate the under-sea link till the year 2086.

Cyclists can use the Eurotunnel Shuttle to travel between Great Britain and France, with the bicycles being housed in specially adapted trailers and the cyclists travelling in a minibus. Lorries are carried on semi-open wagons, with a separate passenger carriage for the drivers. *Eurotunnel* also earns toll revenue from train operators (Eurostar for rail passengers, and EWS and SNCF for rail freight) which use the Tunnel. A one way standard ticket costs UK £49 (~Euro 62), with discounts and free-bees offered to frequent travelers. Train travel between London

---

[7]   *1985 prices, construction costs only.*
[8]   *www.eurotunnel.com*

and Paris takes three hours, while between London and Brussels, takes two hours and forty five minutes. London and cities in Scotland and Wales are also connected by train to cities in Germany, Switzerland and other countries on the European mainland.

With more than 300 trains running in a day, the channel has provided passage to over 2.1 million cars and 1.4 million trucks in 2007 alone, while aggregating in excess of 215 million passengers since commissioning in 1994.

Eurotunnel has admitted that it faces "fundamental" financial difficulties and has consistently struggled to meet interest payments due on its debt. For instance, a default of on the UK £ 8.0 billion junior debt in 1995, triggered one of the largest restructuring efforts in corporate history, involving a syndicate of more than 220 banks[9]. Passenger numbers through the tunnel have never lived up to expectations. Eurostar trains carry about 6 million passengers a year compared to original forecasts of 16 million, (1994 population approx 58 million each for UK and France). Crossing the channel through the tunnel consumes 35 minutes as opposed to 75 minutes by ferry. Ferries have failed to die the death some experts had predicted, while budget airlines have made flying between the UK and the mainland a more attractive option.

Consequent to debt restructuring efforts, of the total debt of Euro 4.13 billion, the annual interest payout stands at about Euro 229 million with the first installment of principal being payable in 2013. Figure 1 indicates that contrary to projections (and revisions) actual revenues have failed to grow post 1999. Recent trends, however, have been marginally more encouraging. The company broke-even in 2007, earning Euro 500 million in shuttle service revenue alone, reaching total revenues of Euro 775 million and an EBITDA of Euro 439 million. The group reported a net profit of Euro 1 million[10]. Results announced for the first half of calendar year 2008 indicate an increase

---

[9]   Vilanova, Laurent *"Financial Distress, Lender Passivity and Project Finance: The Case of Eurotunnel"*, Working paper, University of Lyon, France.

[10]   *2007 Summary financial statements released by the company.*

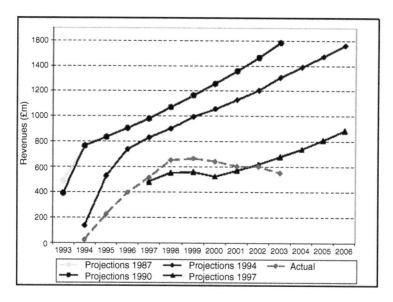

Figure 1: Projections made at various stages compared to the actual financial performance of Eurotunnel.

in numbers of Eurostar passengers (18%), trucks (7%), cars (4%) and coaches (5%) but a decline in rail freight (7%). Eurotunnel has reported a net profit of Euro 26 m for the reporting period.

Ownership patterns

Some analysts have argued that the essence of project finance being concentrated ownership, Eurotunnel's financial distress is on account of distributed ownership of shares among a large number of individual shareholders, each holding too few shares to exert sufficient pressure on management or to effectively negotiate with lenders etc. The details of Eurotunnel shareholding are presented in Annexures 3 and 4 to this case. Observers believe that the construction companies and other contractors designed long-term contracts which were unfavourable to the operating company, and the dispersed shareholders could not defend their interests. It is also argued that despite being illiquid for prolonged spells, the lender banks did not trigger bankruptcy proceedings owing to the highly specified assets owned by Eurotunnel – and the banks could not divert these assets to more efficient and revenue-yielding applications. When the banks took active positions on the project company's board, they could still not prevent the opportunistic behaviour of the construction companies, as they lacked the necessary technical expertise[11].

Environmental Concerns

Once complete, the tunnel was slated to reduce air, water and noise pollution by replacing air craft and ferries with trains and by combining road and rail traffic. However, activists have pointed to the disturbance caused to the sea floor and disruption to sea life during construction. Issues relating to depositing plowed through chalk have been debated.

Eurotunnel has established an environment management system conforming to the stipulations of the ISO 14001 standard. In the year 2007, Eurotunnel published its carbon footprint, taking into account, its operations in the UK and in France, electricity required for traction power for shuttles, Eurostar and freight trains, workshop activity, Diesel works locomotives, road vehicles used for employee conveyance, catering etc.

Issues for Discussion

From the foregoing discussion it is evident that two infrastructure projects, each linking two members of the European Union otherwise separated by geography, have met with substantially different market responses, and consequently one enjoys superior financial health compared to the other. Project analysts are required to identify patterns to help optimize projects in the future.

---

[11]   *Laurent Vilanova "Financial Distress, Lender Passivity and Project Finance: The Case of Eurotunnel", Working paper, University of Lyon, September 2006.*

1. "Static cash-flow evaluation techniques underestimate the real value of projects."[12] Considering the real options for expansion, contraction, abandonment etc. could provide for more informed decision-making.

2. The *Sound Link* project forms part of a network and hence "network effects" enhance its prospects.

3. Conversely, the *Eurotunnel* project terminates on the island and does not benefit from being a part of a network.

4. Success of a project depends on spill over effects and evolving circumstances which would need to be estimated *ex-ante*.

5. Inappropriate capital structure and ownership patterns could drive a project into bankruptcy.

---

[12] *Michael Bowe and Ding Lun Lee, "Project evaluation in the presence of multiple embedded real options: evidence from the Taiwan High-Speed Rail Project", Journal of Asian Economics, 15 (2004) p 71–98.*

Annexure 1: Ownership structure of the Oresund Link

Annexure 2: Financial performance of the Oresund Link

(Source: http://osb.oeresundsbron.dk/news/news.php?obj=6181&menu=642)

DKK million	2003	2004	2005	2006	2007
Road traffic revenue	598	668	729	820	934
Rail revenue	403	408	412	421	429
Other revenue	20	11	13	10	16
Total revenue	**1.021**	**1.087**	**1.154**	**1.251**	**1.379**
Operating costs	282	269	276	281	304
Profit before depreciation and financial items	**739**	**818**	**878**	**970**	**1.075**
Depreciation	320	322	322	324	337
Net financing costs	780	676	697	759	827
Result before value adjustment	**–361**	**–180**	**–141**	**–113**	**–89**
Value adjustment, exchange rate effect, net	19	6	21	5	127
Value adjustment, fair value effect, net	344	–453	–423	677	480
Profit/loss for the year	**2**	**–627**	**–543**	**569**	**518**

Annexure 3: Shareholding pattern for Eurotunnel
(Source:http://www.eurotunnel.com/ukcP3Main/ukcCorporate/ukcFinancialData/
ukcFinancialStructure/ukpShareholderAnalysis)

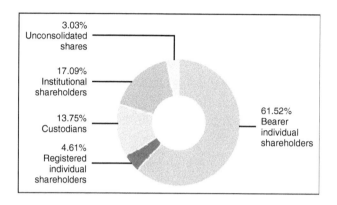

Annexure 4: Distribution of shares among Eurotunnel shareholders
(Source:http://www.eurotunnel.com/ukcP3Main/ukcCorporate/ukcFinancialData/
ukcFinancialStructure/ukpShareholderAnalysis)

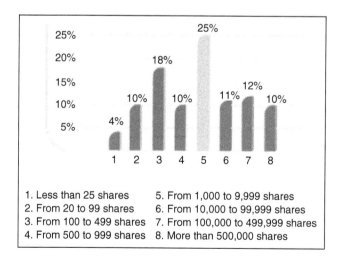

Annexure 5: Eurotunnel shareprice movement on the London Stock Exchange

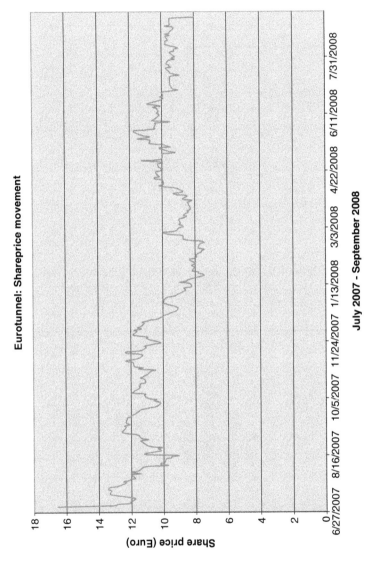

Eurotunnel: Shareprice movement

ANNEXURES

Preliminary Project Information

Objective

The Preliminary information is intended solely as a summary of the proposed project and is to be followed up with detailed financial modeling, legal and financial due diligence and documentation. This report is prepared by a project analyst based on the documents and representations submitted by the project company and from published sources. The claims made are verified as a part of the due diligence investigation.

Confidentiality

The project described in this report, including its existence is generally kept confidential. The information is provided solely to introduce the project to potential equity investors and lenders and is not to be disclosed to any third party. Such disclosures could erode the competitive advantage of the project.

[Other Disclosures and Disclaimers]

Preliminary Project Information

[NAME OF THE INVESTOR / LENDER]
Dated: dd/mm/yyyy

PROJECT DESCRIPTION

Name
Address
Post code / place
Country
Phone/fax number
Webpage
Legal form
Contact person / e_mail address
Sector of industry
Kind of initiative
Facility sought
Prepared By

Preliminary Project Information
[Name of the Project]

1. Background [150 – 200 words]
     i) Incorporation
    ii) History and Credentials
   iii) Key attributes
    iv) Clearances and approvals received
     v) Environmental Impact

2. Ownership/management [100 – 150 words]
     i) Brief introduction to promoters
    ii) Shareholding pattern
   iii) Professional Experience
    iv) Key Management Personnel & Professional Experience
     v) Outsourcing arrangements if any

3. Project Description [400 – 500 words]
     i) Overview of project
    ii) Technology to be employed and Experience with Technology
   iii) Licenses and approvals: fuel, water, land, power supply, off-take
    iv) Contracts executed / planned
     v) Strengths of Project
    vi) Status of Financing

4. Market, competition and target group(s) [200 – 250 words]
     i) Market segment
    ii) Present and Potential competition for project
   iii) Preservation of Monopoly rights, if applicable

5. Financial Highlights [briefly]
    i) Project Size   :
    ii) Project Cost   : [ ] USD (approx local currency)
    iii) Capital Structure   : [D/E]
    iv) Capacity Factor   : [ ] % [at specified point in time]
6. Future Projects / Expansion [100 – 200 words]
    i) Prospects for expanding existing project, vertical integration
    ii) Prospects for acquiring other projects
    iii) Prospects for diversification

7. Risk factors / Issues [200 – 250 words]
    i) [Capacity of Sponsors / Management to implement and operate project]
    ii) [Management of growth and diversification]
    iii) [Delays in receiving statutory clearances and regulatory approvals]
    iv) [Other issues]

ಙಬ

Investment Proposal
[Total text: max 8 pages + Financial statements annexed]
Date: dd/mm/yyyy

Company Name	:	[Name of the company]
Place & Country	:	
Contact Person	:	[Name and e_mail address]
Proposed Project	:	[Brief introduction to project]
Total Project Cost	:	[ ] USD & [ ] local currency
Capital Structure	:	[D/E]

Quantum of Equity Sought	:
Face Value and Premium	:
Number of Shares	:
Shareholding Proportion offered	:
Proposed tenure of shareholding	:
Exit Strategy	:
Valuation at Exit	:
Ex-Ante Return Expectations	:
Key Protections and Preferences	:

Investment Proposal

1. Project Summary [200 - 250 words]

2. Background Information [300 - 400 words]
   a. Evolution of project
   b. Present status
   c. Proposed operations

3. Ownership / Management [300 - 400 words]
   a. Shareholding pattern and promoters' experience
   b. Introduction of top management
   c. Outsourcing relationships

4. Market [300 – 350 words]
   a. Nature of product or service to be delivered
   b. Organization of the industry and competitive advantage
   c. Pricing strategies

5. Competition [300 – 350 words]
   a. Existing competition / Anticipated entry
   b. Licensing conditions and Regulatory safeguards

6. Financial Model [400 – 500 words]
   a. Discussion of input parameters
   b. Discussion of debt funding secured / sought
   c. Discussion of shareholding offered and returns expected
   d. Sensitivity and scenario analyses
   e. Risk management measures and costs involved

Approval Note: Investment Proposal
(Total text: max 4 pages + Financial statements annexed, if applicable)
Date: dd/mm/yyyy

Assessment of Project and Approval of Investment

Company Name   :

Place & Country   :

Contact Person   :

Project Objective   :

Total Project Cost   :

Capital Structure   :

Equity investment approved [USD]   :

Face Value / Premium / % Shareholding   :

Disbursement   :

Tenure   :

Exit Strategy / Valuation   :

Key Observations and conditions precedent :

Recommendation   :

Approval Note: Investment Proposal

1. Project Summary

2. Requested Investment

3. Risks / Issues / Concerns

4. Recommendation / Approval (subject to conditions precedent)

ಬಿಂಬ

DEBT PROPOSAL
(Total text: max 8 pages + Financial statements annexed)
Date: dd/mm/yyyy

Company Name   : {name of the company}

Place & Country   :

Contact Person and e_mail address   : {name of contact person}

Project Objective   :

Total Project Cost   :

Capital Structure   : {D/E}

Principal Shareholders   : {shareholding pattern}

Quantum of Debt Sought   :

Special Arrangements (if any)   : {currencies, imports, swaps etc.}

Tenure   :

Disbursement Schedule

Purpose   :

Interest Rate   :

Repayment Pattern   : {equated / balloon / other}

Security offered   : {description of project assets}

Minimum DSCR   : {likely case / worst case}

Debt Proposal

1. Project Summary [200 - 250 words]

2. Background Information [300 - 400 words]
    a. Evolution of project
    b. Present status
    c. Proposed operations

3. Ownership / Management [300 - 400 words]
    a. Shareholding pattern and promoters' experience
    b. Introduction of top management
    c. Outsourcing relationships

4. Market [300 – 350 words]
    a. Nature of product or service to be delivered
    b. Organization of the industry and competitive advantage
    c. Pricing strategies

5. Competition [300 – 350 words]
    a. Existing competition / Anticipated entry
    b. Licensing and Regulatory safeguards

6. Financial Model [400 – 500 words]
    a. Discussion of input parameters
    b. Discussion of equity funding secured / sought and terms
    c. Discussion of debt funding sought and terms
        i. Quantum of debt
        ii. Tenure of debt
        iii. Disbursement Schedule
        iv. Interest rate

        v. Repayment pattern
       vi. DSCR (best, likely and worst case)
     vii. Security on offer
    viii. Currency issues
  d. Sensitivity and scenario analyses

7. Risk management measures including insurance contracts and costs involved.

ೲಐ

Approval Note: Debt Proposal
(Total text: max 4 pages + Financial statements annexed, if applicable)
Date: dd/mm/yyyy

Assessment of Project and Sanction of Debt

Company Name   :

Place & Country   :

Contact Person   :

Project Objective   :

Total Project Cost   :

Capital Structure   :

Shareholding   :

Quantum of Debt   :

Disbursement   :

Tenure   :

Interest Rate   :

Repayment Pattern   :

Security   :

Key Observations and conditions precedent :

Recommendation   :

Approval Note: Debt Proposal

1. Project Summary

2. Requested Debt

3. Risks / Issues / Concerns

4. Recommendation / Approval (subject to conditions precedent)

৪০৫৪

Index

For Product Safety Concerns and Information please contact our EU
representative GPSR@taylorandfrancis.com
Taylor & Francis Verlag GmbH, Kaufingerstraße 24, 80331 München, Germany

www.ingramcontent.com/pod-product-compliance
Ingram Content Group UK Ltd.
Pitfield, Milton Keynes, MK11 3LW, UK
UKHW021608240425
457818UK00018B/450